SH
BAT
DRESS
SINCE 1945

C000128408

BRITISH
COMBAT
DRESS
SINCE 1945

MICHAEL G. BURNS

1. Near Lemgo, Germany in 1960, John Humber (left) and Michael Harrsion of 1st Battalion A&SH plan their next move. Humber carries an A41 on a GS carrier and wears a headset/handset piece – the headset over his ears, the operator handset dangling on his chest – while Harrison uses the tele-handset to communicate. Their ammo boots and gaiters are shown to advantage. Gaiters, or anklets, were made of web canvas and had two leather straps with brass buckles. [A&SH]

ARMS AND
ARMOUR

Arms and Armour Press
A Cassell Imprint
Villiers House, 41–47 Strand, London WC2N 5JE.

Distributed in the USA by Sterling Publishing Co. Inc., 387 Park
Avenue South, New York, NY 10016-8810.

Distributed in Australia by Capricorn Link (Australia) Pty. Ltd, P.O.
Box 665, Lane Cove, New South Wales 2066.

British Library Cataloguing in Publication Data
Burns, Michael G., *1953–*
British combat dress since 1945
I. Title
355.140941
ISBN 0-85368-984-9

Designed and edited by DAG Publications Ltd. Designed by David
Gibbons; edited by Michael Boxall; layout by Anthony A. Evans;
typeset by Ronset Typesetters, Darwen, Lancashire; camerawork by
M&E Reproductions, North Fambridge, Essex; printed and bound in
Great Britain by The Bath Press, Avon.

2

To
Lieutenant-Colonel James Heaton,
RAMC, 1912–1990

INTRODUCTION

Although battledress had been in service with British and Commonwealth armed forces for eight years by the time the Second World War ended in August 1945, it still had the better part of its service to go.

For two decades, the 1940s and 1950s, battledress was the temperate climate field uniform of the British Army. British factories produced five patterns of battledress. US factories produced a sixth. Canadian and Commonwealth factories in Australia, New Zealand and South Africa also produced battledress in distinctive patterns, worn by Commonwealth soldiers, and, particularly the Canadian pattern, by the British Army. The many patterns of battledress underwent modification, official and unofficial. Moreover, despite its faults, battledress was extensively copied during and after the war by both friend and foe. Germany, France, Belgium, Holland and Denmark all produced a form of battledress for field or parade purposes.

For most British Army other ranks of the Second World War, battledress was the universal uniform for parade, walking-out, working and fighting. Army officers and all ranks of the other services had alternative uniforms, and would use battledress as a working-dress alternative to their jacketed service dress. With the abolition of National Service in the 1950s, the new British regular army adopted a form of service dress (No. 2 Dress) for parade wear and combat dress for the field. Shortly afterwards, the Territorial Army followed suit.

Origins in Experience

Britain's long succession of colonial wars, particularly in India and South Africa, led to the development of a neutral-coloured, loose-fitting, practical field uniform. The modern era in field uniform began with the Third

2. In Berlin, a Comet from the Independent Tank Squadron, RTR, giving troops of 1st Battalion, A&SH a lift at the conclusion of the Brigade Exercise 'Minor Seas II', 3 November 1955. This photograph shows almost everything being worn with post-war battledress and 1938-pattern equipment. [A&SH]

5

Boer War (1899–1902) which the British Army fought entirely in khaki because rifle fire had become so accurate that the wearing of coloured clothing might shorten a soldier's life. Utilitarian 'slouch' or 'bush' hats became almost universal. The twin pouches were awkward for prone firing – before soldiers rarely had to fire lying down – and cartridge bandoliers were favoured. Replacing the valise in fighting order kit, a haversack was worn on the shoulders, a practice which continues to the present.

As usual after a large war there was much revision, and from 1902 the temporary use of khaki in South Africa was confirmed when khaki service dress became a general issue for training and general duties. It consisted of a round cap, khaki serge jacket and trousers and puttees, with the old buff leather equipment, coloured with khaki blanco. For service in hot climates, a lighter, cotton drill material was approved. Polishing of 'bright-work' had to continue.

Full dress was retained for ceremonial duties, reviews, church parades, guards, etc., but was entirely useless in war. Henceforth, a soldier trained and worked in the same kit he would wear on active service. Finally, 1914 ended general use of full dress. Thereafter, it was confined to Household Troops, bands and officers at levees. However, 'walking-out' dress for an infantryman consisted of the full dress tunic, or doublet, and trousers or kilt, forage cap or Glengarry, with waist belt, swagger cane and gloves.

Following the invention of charger-loading in the early 1900s, the short rifle was introduced in 1908, and the polished leather ammunition pouches and accoutrements gave way to scientifically designed webbing equipment, including pack and haversack (except for mounted soldiers who kept the leather bandolier). The new cartridge bandolier had small pouches each holding three charges.

This, the first 'all-in-one' webbing equipment, was far less tiring to wear, because the weight was no longer distributed by straps crossing the chest, and could be donned or shed in seconds. However, if the 1908 uniform were easier to wear and abolished the pipe-clay days, webbing equipment had to be blancoed green and brass still had to shine. Puttees remained, too; they gave good protection to the lower legs, but were irksome to wind on correctly.

Although universal khaki service dress was first introduced in 1902, it was not until 1913 that it became obligatory for all ranks on all occasions except full dress. This was the field dress in which the British Army went to war in August 1914, but in 1915, leather equipment was hastily manufactured to equip 'Kitchener's' battalions. The leather braces would stretch when they got wet until the pack hung on the backside (as in 1873). The equipment was replaced by webbing as quickly as possible.

The service dress for ORs consisted of a single-breasted khaki serge tunic with stand-and-fall collar, five metal general service pattern buttons in front, patch breast and side pockets with flap and button, and matching rounded shoulder-straps. Pantaloons in khaki serge for unmounted and Bedford cord for mounted personnel were worn with black ankle boots and khaki puttees. The OR's greatcoat was single-breasted.

Officers' service dress comprised a modern open khaki serge tunic with lapels, light khaki shirt and tie, matching khaki pantaloons, puttees and brown ankle boots, or long khaki trousers with brown shoes. Officers in mounted units, and mounted officers in unmounted units, as well as staff and general officers, could also wear cord breeches and brown leather field boots. The officer's greatcoat was double-breasted.

During the Great War, headgear included the M. 1916 helmet (Mark I), stiff peaked service cap, and the side cap (Cap, FS, or 'fore and aft'). Some regiments and corps kept distinctive head-dress. At the end of the war large stocks of clothing and equipment were held in ordnance stores, sufficient to meet the needs of the small peace-time British Army for many years.

In the early 1930s, the War Office became increasingly aware of the need for a new and more rational combat dress to succeed field uniform. Research to improve field uniforms was undertaken on a small scale, mainly to meet the needs of 'mechanization'. Over several years experiments included deerstalker hats, bush jackets and (tested by units in 1932) gaiters. As early as 1933–4, trials were run with a two-piece suit of blouse and trousers and short anklets. The design of the new battle suit had been developed by 1937, and it was tested by some regular units that year.

For the first time, the soldier was given a specifically designed active service dress. Two designs of field uniform were shown to the Press in 1938, both made up in denim. One was very similar to Australian service dress, which had already undergone troop trials in drab serge. The other design was modelled on the fashionable skiing clothing, a short jacket blouse and baggy trousers gathered at the ankles. It was the latter that was developed into battledress.

It was found that denim was too light for the north-western European climate so the 'ski-suit' was made up in the drab serge of the existing service dress and named 'Battledress, Serge'. Serge is a twill-worsted cloth used for dress, coat and suit making.

Conscript Suits

In May 1939, Parliament passed a Bill under which every man of 20 years and over had to register for two years' military service, producing the first militia drafts, and a massive effort to clothe them would be required. The new 'battledress' began to replace the service dress in April 1939; the first to receive it were the first National Servicemen called up from the militia early that summer. Quantity manufacture of battledress began in 1939, rendering service dress obsolete. The first specification was No. E/1037 of 28 October 1938, which was modified as necessary.

Prototypes of battledress patterns were made by the Garment Development Section (GDS), Royal Dockyard, Woolwich. All clothing made up by GDS carried its initials. Contracting clothing manufacturers were invited to tender for producing battledress in quantity against official specifications issued by the Chief Inspector of Stores and Clothing [CISC] (this title contracted to Chief Inspector of Clothing [CIC] in 1939, which became a Director post [DIC] post-war).

With war imminent, on 2 September 1939 the National Service (Armed Forces) Bill went before Parliament, calling up all able-bodied men between 18 and 41 for active service 'for the duration of hostilities'. Once war had begun, both service dress and battledress were worn on active service until stocks of the latter became available in sufficient quantity to re-equip all troops in the spring of 1940. By the end of 1940, battledress had replaced service dress as the field uniform of the British Army.

In 1938, the final pattern was authorized for all arms, except for the few remaining horsed cavalry regiments. The original, waist-length single-breasted blouse was made of a rough serge with stand-and-fall collar, fly front, two pleated breast patch pockets with flap and concealed button (the buttons were made of a vegetable compound and were green) and one inner pocket. At the waist the blouse was gathered into a waistband and fastened with a flat metal buckle on the right of centre. For security, all distinctions and insignia were deleted.

The trousers were straight and were generously fitted with the normal side and hip pockets plus an awkwardly placed, large pocket with flap on the left front thigh to contain a map and a sealed pleated pocket on the right front just below the waist. At the bottoms the trousers had a tab and button, so they could be fastened around the ankle for wear with black leather ankle boots and web anklets.

The blouse was cut on very easy fitting lines. The back was cut with a raised centre back seam which was raised well up on top of the shoulder, and there were no sideseams. The front joined the neck, finishing with a Panteen collar. The left forepart terminated down the centre of the front. Five brass, four-holed buttons in a fly fastened the front, and two hooks and eyes the front of the standing collar. The waist section was gathered into a 2in wide waistbelt, which extended to the left into a 9in strap which buckled at the side waist. The sleeves, again moder-

ately full, were finished with a 3in-wide band into which the upper part was tucked, with a vent in the hind-arm with a buttonhole under a fly. There were standard shoulder-straps. There were patch pockets on each breast, 6 inches deep by 7 inches wide, with a 1¼in box pleat in the centre. The flaps over these pockets were 3 inches deep, tapering to 2 inches. The pocket had a button and a buttonhole concealed on an inner flap.

The trousers were cut moderately wide in the leg with plain bottoms. There was a 1½in wide strap in the leg seam half an inch from the bottom, reaching the front crease where it was buttoned when gaiters were not worn. When gaiters were worn, it pulled over to button on the sideseam. On the left leg there was a patch pocket with a flap, 7 inches wide and 11 inches deep, positioned about 9 inches from the waist and 1½ inches from the fly. The flap covered a buttonhole in the lining. The flap was placed 1 inch above the patch of the pocket. The flap was 3 inches deep, tapering to 2 inches. On the right leg was a 4½in wide, 6in long patch pocket, with a flat pleat in the centre, and positioned 6 inches from the top and 1 inch from the fly. There were side pockets and a hip pocket with a flap and a buttonhole in the lining to conceal the button. The brace buttons were concealed inside the tops.

A new greatcoat pattern, similar to the officers' pattern, superseded both previous patterns. Raincoats were an officer's privilege – ORs used groundsheets in rain!

The original head-dress was a very unmilitary floppy deerstalker's hat but this was replaced by the 'Cap, Field Service' (the gravity-defying sidehat), then in 1943 by the 'Cap, General Service', and the beret. During the Second World War there were few categories of headgear but dozens of variations. Officers wore the khaki service dress cap, with khaki-covered peak, brown leather strap and badge of regiment, corps or organization. ORs of most units continued to wear the khaki field service cap (Cap, FS).

The Cap FS was unsatisfactory. It was difficult to wear at the correct angle, and difficult to keep on in even light breezes or during drill; hair grease permeated it; and it gave no protection from the elements – it could be (but seldom was) turned into a balaclava by folding down the buttoned side-pieces and front peak. With Tommy's genius for vulgar description, the vulvar-shaped thing was re-named! But it was meant only for drill and walking-out and soldiers donned a 'tin hat' on active service.

In 1943, the General Service Cap gradually replaced the FS Cap. The GS Cap was made of several pieces of cloth with a separate headband, like a Balmoral without the tourrie. At unit level officers could wear the regimentally coloured No. 1 Dress Cap. Officers and ORs of Scottish regiments wore the Glengarry bonnet or Tam o' Shanter (TOS), the 'Balmoral' bonnet.

Like service dress, the new uniform began life as a loose-fitting, practical garment, and was 'smartened-up' in later patterns, thus losing much of its original suitability as a dress for combat. It was the nearest thing to a mechanic's overall, symbolic of the mechanized era. 'Spit and polish' had been abandoned but could men feel like soldiers in it? As a working suit, though, it was comfortable and had many good points.

Battledress was acknowledged as being a more practical attire than service dress for active service, but it was widely criticized. Traditionalists complained that it was difficult for a man to look smart and soldierlike in such working garb, but more seriously, the short blouse was generally criticized for giving no protection to the most vulnerable part of the anatomy, the loins, and if, as often happened, buttons flew off at the back, a man was left with a chilling gap just where he needed warmth. A man with a long back found it almost impossible to keep the blouse and trousers together when bending over or stretching.

In 1940 battledress manufacture was simplified by doing away with the pocket pleats and concealed buttons on the blouse, so that five buttons appeared in front and one on each pocket flap and shoulder strap.

Black leather, hob-nail studded, ankle boots of the previous regulation issue pattern, 'Boots, Ammunition', were worn with battledress. All soldiers were issued with two pairs of ammunition boots. One pair was dubbined to make them waterproof and was worn for drill and training. The other pair was kept for 'best' and had to be highly polished. These were reserved for guard duty, and ceremonial and special parades. Some officers continued to wear brown leather boots, according to regimental custom and practice. (Officers' boots were polished brown from 1902, but other ranks continued to wear black.)

Webbing anklets, known as 'gaiters', were approved for wear with battledress in 1938; old-style puttees were rarely worn. Leather anklets were later introduced, and were popular with the Home Guard. In tropical climates hosetops were sometimes worn with battledress.

All clothing was issued. It included collarless 'shirts angola drab' worn with shirt-sleeve order, 'drawers cellular', 'drawers woollen', 'vests woollen', 'gloves woollen' and 'jerseys, pullover'. Toiletry included 'razor, safety' and 'brush, shaving' as the British soldier had to be clean-shaven at all times.

Winter clothing was restricted to these woollen items. When worn with woollen underwear, socks,

3. 'C' Squadron, 13/18th Royal Hussars with their Sherman medium tanks, pause somewhere in north-west Europe in 1944. From 1940, the black beret that RTR had worn since 1924 was authorized for the other mechanized cavalry regiments of the RAC who were also authorized to wear it with regimental badges. It was not evenly issued and some cavalry tank regiments still wore the cap FS for some time. Then, post-war, the RTR claimed exclusive right to the black beret; the rest of the RAC adopted dark blue. [13th/18th Hussars]

shirt and pullover, battledress provided good protection in cold weather and reasonable protection in wet weather. A woollen balaclava could be worn under the steel helmet.

There was also a sand-coloured 'Tropal' coat, first issued to troops in Norway; a stiff, heavy guard coat for sentries, was not intended to be worn in action. A famous relic of the trenches, a leather jerkin, was also issued. The duffle coat also turned up in Italy during the last two winters of the war. In north-west Europe extensive use was made of white snow smocks and helmet covers, but primarily for camouflage, not warmth. Troops would wear denim overalls over the battledress for warmth.

Women's battledress was first issued in 1941 to the ATS for women serving in mixed AA units and as convoy drivers and ambulance drivers, and later for service in overseas (non-tropical) areas. It followed the 1938 male pattern; in late 1942, austerity measures were introduced. Other women's organizations issued it included QARANC, Women's Transport Service (FANY); Mechanized Transport Service; American Ambulance in Great Britain; Anglo-French Ambulance Corps; ENSA and NAAFI. The Women's Auxiliary Air Force (WAAF) had battledress from April 1941 when they were first worn on barrage balloon sites. The pattern followed the airmen's No. 2 Dress, a similarity that continued post-war, the 'Blouse No. 2 (Home) Dress, WRAF' being a scaled-down counterpart of the male blouse except that the torso was fully-lined.

From early in the war, battledress was impregnated with anti-gas chemicals against vesicant vapour. The impregnant – one chemical for temperate, another for tropical climates – reacted with the vapour to neutralize it. The process was discontinued in September 1945. Treated suits – thirteen million! – were a lighter, greyer shade. The chemicals smelt awful so soldiers would walk in the rain to rinse them out – although this often turned the suits bile-green!

In Service

The original battledress was intended to be a loose-fitting and comfortable field uniform under which further layers of clothing could be worn according to the weather. A soldier's comfort, not appearance, was the primary consideration: when it was introduced, battledress was intended to be worn only on active service; service dress was to be retained for use in barracks, rear areas, walking-out and parade.

When battledress became the only temperate uniform issued to troops, two suits per man, the practice of using one suit for 'best' wear became universal. The 'best' suit was tailored to smart, usually slim fit, cheered up with coloured insignia, and altered, shaved, shaped and pressed into shapes far removed from the baggy 'ski-suit'.

Originally officers were permitted to have their battledress made up by military tailors, in various materials, styles and fit, but the practice did not persist for long. In line with war economy, officers were ordered to wear issue-pattern battledress. Other than rank insignia, only the open neck, collared-shirt in khaki and tie marked out officers – and brown leather gloves and shoes, and a swagger stick. This did not prevent officers having both their 'best' and 'active service' suits subtly re-tailored to a more comfortable, smart, individual fit.

Regular drill sergeants thought the uniform made men look like garage mechanics. It was not possible to keep a crease in the trousers in the prescribed manner for there were capacious pockets just where the front creases should be. There were not even any metal buttons to polish! There were, of course, still the black leather boots with their metal eyelets to shine.

Conversely, and perversely, most NCOs and WOs considered that battledress should be worn as issued, and quickly overruled any attempt to smarten it up by re-tailoring, facing collars, pressing creases and pleats. But eradicating incipient subversion was an uphill task. The private soldier, neither wishing to be mistaken for a recruit nor to reduce his chances with the girls at or after a dance, resisted such regimentation and strove to express individuality. Deprived of the right to wear civilian clothes, he did his best to achieve a distinctive appearance with a uniform that could do its best to make him look like a mobile sack of potatoes.

There was another alternative that became available to enterprising Tommies later as manufacture of battledress in the USA, Canada and Australia got under way. British soldiers recognized the superior qualities of cloth, cut and finish of US, Australian and Canadian suits. During the war, US 'Battle Dress' was much sought after by British soldiers, including senior officers, and Canadian suits were worn by British soldiers whenever they could get hold of them. Post-war stocks of Canadian suits in British stores were issued to British units after the Canadian Army withdrew from the Middle East and Europe and it was common to see British soldiers wearing it in the later 1940s. In the 1950s, stocks of the superior Australian battledress became available and were eagerly sought after by British troops.

Collar and Tie

It had only been in 1920 that the officer's privilege of wearing civilian clothes – 'mufti' – on leave or when 'walking out' was officially extended to warrant officers and senior NCOs. In 1946, that privilege was allowed to private soldiers and junior NCOs as well. Wearing plain clothes was only allowed in Britain. In overseas stations, uniform had to be worn at all times on or off duty. In the heat of India, day walking-out

4. A King's Own Gurkha Officer, company 2ic Subadar Lilabur Rana, and his three platoon commanders discuss orders in a trench south of the River Senio, Italy, before an assault in January 1945. On battledress, NCOs had one to three white rank chevrons on both sleeves. Officers wore embroidered rank insignia on both shoulder-straps: company officers had one to three pips and field officers a crown and one to three pips; generals had crossed baton, sword and pip, or one crown, or one pip and crown, and field marshals had crossed batons in a laurel wreath surmounted by a crown. Senior officers (substantive colonel and above) wore red cap bands and gorget patches. The 1939–45 helmet was the same as that worn during the 1914–18 war, but had rubber shock absorbers and an easily detachable lining. Also shown are a pair of Mk V binoculars and a Thompson SMG. [Gurkhas]

dress was shirt-sleeve order, sleeves of the KD shirts neatly rolled to just above the elbow, shorts and puttees for dismounted units, slacks for mounted. After dusk, sleeves were rolled down and all units wore slacks – a precaution against mosquito bites.

Despite the unpromising nature of the basic battle-dress suit, the more determined soldiers had created a variety of individual, more fashionable stylings within a few months of being issued with it. Unlike officers, ORs did not have the advantages of tailors and clothing coupons, but unit tailors whose task it was to fit issue blouses to individuals, by making diagonal tucks above the breast pockets, and putting a seam in the back of the neck to fit collars, might be persuaded to go farther. Fewer, but wider pleats in the rear of the blouse above the waistband could be pressed to fan out in a wheatsheaf. Shoulders might be padded and triangular gussets inserted to give a 'flare' to trousers, to accord with street fashion. But it was collars and ties that liberated battledress!

Within weeks of the appearance of collars and ties among the soldiery, there had been a chaotic series of modifications aimed at defeating the tendency of the drill lining material, now visible at the collar of the blouse, to become filthy after a week or two of wear. Some scrubbed it regularly, making the material threadbare and faded. It could be bleached with toothpaste, with interesting results in the rain! Soldiers risked a charge by having local civilian tailors face the open collar with serge or even alter the collar by cutting stepped lapels. Many unit officers were lenient and some gave resigned approval, with unit orders allowing modifications so long as the collar could still be fastened for parade, that is so long as the

hooks and eyes were retained and a buttonhole was made in the left front, which was virtually impossible with the fly-front of the pre-1942 issue blouse.

The stand-up collar had been designed when soldiers went in fear of sword thrusts to the neck – originally they were of leather and equally resented! The prohibition of collars and ties had been a contentious issue with British soldiers who resented the denial of a right enjoyed by the members of the other services. Ex-civilians did not see why they should look old-fashioned and unstylish when walking out.

In December 1944, an Army Regulation permitted other ranks to open the blouse collar and wear a collar and tie when off duty, though they had to keep the means of closing the collar when on duty. There followed various unofficial alterations in the form of faced lapels like those ordered by officers from their tailors for some years.

The 1946-pattern battledress blouse attempted to regulate the unofficial modifications which thousands of individual soldiers had been ordering from local tailors, in defiance of repeated Part I Unit Orders to the effect that uniforms must not be defaced.

For the open collar, cheap sand-coloured drill ties were issued, but knitted ties were later issued. The collarless KF shirt was superseded by several patterns until a definitive pattern was established in the mid-1950s.

Battledress was not only smart, but no longer anonymous. By 1945, most of the identifying marks and the regimental distinctions so dear to the British soldier that had been worn with service dress had been restored on battledress, at least for parade and ceremonial purposes. At first, they had all been deleted for security, but they served morale better and from 1941, most troops wore a colourful insignia on sleeves and shoulder – arm of service strips above formation sign on sleeves, and sometimes regimental flashes.

Tropical Uniforms

Less effective thought had been given to tropical combat dress than to temperate combat dress, and the Second World War forced many changes in British tropical uniform. During the early campaigns in North Africa, Sicily, the semi-tropical and hot-and-dry Mediterranean climate areas of Greece and Crete British troops fought in khaki drill (KD) shirts and shorts or slacks; in Italy, however, the denim battledress overalls were increasingly used as summer combat dress, particularly by infantry, as more suitable. In the war in tropical and jungle conditions against the Japanese which began in December 1941, the British and Indian Armies at first wore KD, but hastily replaced it with a new tropical uniform, Jungle Green (JG). With the rejection by 1941 of the medical regulations that made spinepads and topees compulsory, caps FS, bonnets, steel helmets and woollen caps were widely worn.

In 1939, standard-issue semi-tropical and tropical field uniform was KD shorts and Aertex collared, long-sleeve shirt, and these remained in service through the war. (One of the stranger items were Bombay Bloomers, three-quarter length KD shorts whose legs could be buttoned-up or let down and tucked into the boottop to protect from malarial mosquitoes, but mainly against blister gases which it was thought likely the Japanese would use).

By early 1943, however, British factories were producing a more practical field uniform, trousers and a 'bush jacket' of khaki drill material, not Aertex and

thus more durable. KD jacket, shirt and long trousers (cotton cord for mounted personnel) or shorts and ammo boots or canvas shoes with rubber soles were common in the Mediterranean areas.

At first the British soldiers who struggled against the Japanese assaults in the Far East in 1941–2 wore KD field uniform of shorts and shirt, a uniform that was rapidly found entirely unsuitable to the climate and jungle of South-East Asia. Khaki, perfect for desert warfare, was entirely wrong for the jungle so existing stocks of KD trousers and khaki Aertex shirts were dyed green as a temporary measure.

In 1942, a more practical form of jungle warfare dress was designed, consisting of a JG Aertex battledress blouse and JG drill battledress trousers; a JG Aertex bush jacket was produced as an alternative to the blouse. These three Indian Pattern items, made up by Indian clothing factories, were the main field uniform worn in the Far East until 1945. Canvas shoes and jungle hats became standard issue. The bush or slouch hat of the Boer War, at first limited to Australian and New Zealand troops, soon became the most popular headdress. JG became black with sweat minutes after putting it on.

After the end of the European war, British clothing factories began to produce new styles of JG uniform for issue to the reinforcements being sent to the Far East. The US Army field uniform in use in the Pacific was taken as a basis; many features of the American OD herringbone twill trousers and jacket were incorporated into the new-style uniform. The British rejected Aertex and returned to drill for both the jacket and trousers. The suit had a 'gas flap' across the chest, and anti-gas cuffs. The trousers resembled battledress in design, the jacket was very similar to the US item. The new attire was termed Olive Green (OG) uniform. Two patterns were made, the second using the recently available synthetic materials.

With these British pattern uniforms came various items designed specifically for the Far East. These included mosquito nets for head and hands, canvas and rubber jungle boots based on US items, lightweight green blankets and JG puttees. The end of the Far East war meant most of these items went into ordnance stores to be issued post-war.

After world hostilities ceased in 1945, the many items of KD, JG and OG continued to be issued to British troops in the Middle and Far East, and were worn in Palestine, Egypt and Malaya, but by 1950 stocks were running low and a new tropical uniform was introduced in KD and JG. However, the 1950-pattern tropical uniform was poorly designed. Troops tried hard to find earlier KD or JG patterns instead. The Aertex bush jacket had an applied belt which had to be cut off in order to wear equipment, and was a tight, smart but uncomfortable fit. Trousers and shorts fastened at the waist with a pair of cross-over belts which gripped large metal buckles on the hips and these could be very harsh on the march when equipment bore down on them. In contrast, the Gurkha's smart JG uniform, run up by their contractors' tailors, was coveted by others and the final version of the JG uniform was a copy of the Gurkha shirt, replacing the 1950 pattern JG bush shirt.

Post-war hot climate working dress varied but usually involved being stripped to the waist with either KD or OG shorts or slacks. In some cases, the brimmed cotton hat in KD or OG was worn but in other cases the beret. For a time after the war, men in the Far East continued to wear the felt bush hat. In many units the working dress was blue PT shorts and ammo boots with grey socks rolled down over the boot. With no upper garments, all NCOs and WOs wore cotton wrist bands with removable metal badges so that the band could easily be washed. Later, embroidered badges or white cotton cut-outs were used on the green or KD wrist bands so that the whole thing could be washed. In the 1960s or early 1970s, men serving in the Middle East were often seen in suede desert boots. In the Far East, long green canvas rubber-soled jungle boots were issued. A cotton net sweat rag was sometimes worn at the neck under the collar.

Special Combat Dress

Airborne troops were issued with battledress of a modified pattern with enlarged map pockets on the left thigh, and stowage for a fighting knife in the right seam. The first British paratroopers were issued with a copy of the German parachutist's single-breasted cotton smock. By later 1941, they were being issued with the 'Denison' camouflaged smock and rimless steel helmet with leather chin-strap and cup (later, web strap and rubber cup). This was the conception of Captain Denison who served with a camouflage unit commanded by Oliver Messel, the eminent stage designer. For the jump, a loose-fitting sleeveless jump jacket with zip-fastener was worn over the camouflage smock and equipment. The Denison continued in use long after the war – for at least twenty years. 'Although a status symbol in the British Army, the Denison,' wrote ex-SAS officer, Barry Gregory, 'was windproof but not waterproof and stank after use like a coal-miner's sweat shirt. I used it in extremis as a pillow when sleeping out with sleeping-bag and poncho to keep my head above ground level.'

Armoured fighting vehicle crews were also issued with battledress which they wore under a one-piece black denim overall, but they soon adopted standard-issue clothing and the working denims. Practical experience, however, led to the development of a special sand-coloured one-piece overall ('pixie-suit')

with khaki lining and collar, and two zip-fasteners the full length of the front to make it easy to don and shed, and to make it convertible to a sleeping-bag. It was issued in 1944 just before the final winter of the war.

'Denims' were a battledress-style overall suit in varying shades of khaki, introduced with battledress and to be worn over it. They replaced the canvas overalls as the work or fatigue uniform of the British Army. Made of a drab-earth brown denim, to a pattern closely based upon that of battledress, the 1937 pattern was followed by several other types. Denims were lighter than battledress and were often worn from 1943 to 1945 on active service. In warm-weather combat areas they were worn instead of KD – despite being too loose if worn alone. Conversely, in north-west Europe, they were worn over battledress against the cold. Denims were also widely used by AFV crews until special tank crew uniforms were issued. Coveralls – a one-piece suit of overalls – replaced the denims. The first pattern was a heavy denim material but the current pattern are of a lighter cotton material in green. REME metalworking trades wear a heavier blue coverall suit, a naval issue and one more resistant to burning.

The standard issue load-bearing equipment from 1940 to 1960 was the 1937-pattern webbing belt and braces set, with belt pouches and backpacks. For tropical areas, a new set was devised to cope with the conditions, the JG 1944 pattern, essentially similar. The equipment concepts were well-received, although packs came in for some criticism. British mountain warfare troops demanded a rucksack to replace the 1937-pattern pack which they found impracticable. The first rucksack to enter British Army service was the famous Bergen, made of canvas, chrome leather, webbing and steel.

The Bergen first appeared in 1942 together with special clothing, boots and skis to equip the mountain troops training to liberate northern occupied Europe. However, the Bergen's wider application was quickly appreciated and it was adopted by other special duties units, such as Commandos, SAS and SBS. In Italy, it was used by infantry (who also used many US Army rucksacks). In the late 1940s, Bergens were taken from store to equip the re-formed SAS in Malaya. During the post-war years, many became available for use by infantry battalions.

No. 5 Dress

In 1947 the War Office began a radical reconsideration of the Army's dress. A Special Army Order of 13 May stated: 'Consequent on the recommendations of the Committee on Post-War Dress for the Army, considerable changes in dress ... have now been approved.' Tropical dress was considered separately,

5. Eighth Army Gurkhas, with bayonet and kukri, advance over open ground towards the Mareth Line, Libya, in March 1943. In the 1930s research had determined that a 'miniature' bayonet – little longer than a kitchen knife – was all that was needed to kill a man, and would be more handy and lighter than the sword-bladed weapon then on issue. It was introduced together with the Mk IV SMLE, a mass-produced simplified Mk III with changes such as aperture sight, only three rifling grooves and no nose-cap. [Gurkhas]

and new tropical dress regulations became effective from 3 November 1948.

The changes scheduled in May 1947 were the abolition of service dress and the ' . . . introduction of a new uniform for wear by all ranks of the Active Army and the Territorial Army on ceremonial occasions, other parades for which battledress is unsuitable, and for walking out'. This became the blue No. 1 Dress. The War Office said that: 'Battledress will be worn for active service, training and working duties.' This applied to all ranks. Also, mess dress was not currently in use.

The War Office abolished the khaki beret and from 1947 coloured berets were to be worn with battledress: 11th Hussars, brown with a crimson band; RTR, black; AAC and other airborne forces, maroon; rifle regiments, rifle green; light infantry regiments, dark green; all other regiments and corps, dark blue.

The scale of issue was two suits No. 1 Dress, two suits battledress and protective clothing as authorized for officers; ORs received only one No. 1 suit; and the Territorials received only one suit of No. 1 and battledress.

The new pattern of battledress was to be neater and more comfortable:

'The present type will be retained subject to the following modifications:
(a) Increased ventilation.
(b) Wider range of fittings.
(c) Blouse to have pleated breast pockets, fly front and faced lapels.
(d) Material to be the same for officers and other ranks.'

After the Second World War the modified 1949-pattern battledress became the standard issue. The shirt to be worn with the new battledress was to be the coat type with attached collar, breast pockets and shoulder-straps so that it could be worn in shirt-sleeve order.

For home service (a 'Cold Climate Area') battledress was supplied by the RAOC, and was worn by officers with open neck and regulation tie at all times, and with a web belt. Dress requirements varied during the

late 1940s and 1950s, but for much of the period included two suits battledress, two pairs anklets, one beret, George boots, ankle boots, embroidered arm titles or tartan patches, one pullover, one pair braces, one pair cellular and one pair woollen drawers, one or two woollen vests, four pairs worsted socks, one khaki tie, three taffeta lightweight shirts and six collars. (The cost of refitting battledress was included in an officer's uniform allowance.)

Woollen serge battledress was gradually replaced by layered combat dress, which had first been issued to troops in Korea but it did not become generally available until the late 1950s. Battledress was gradually withdrawn during the 1960s. One regiment stopped issuing it to recruits at regimental depots in 1962, although men who had already been issued with one suit kept it until 1963. Other regiments kept No. 5 Dress as barracks dress during the early 1960s, despite the issue of one suit of the new service dress.

Known as 'No. 5 Dress' in a range of Orders of Dress in the British Army, it was not until the late 1960s that issue of battledress ceased, but for some years its use had been limited to orders of working dress, that

6. Battle preparation: men of the 7/9th Royal Scots clean their section weapons and prepare tape between battles during 1944. The white tape was laid to mark safe lanes through minefields, or indicate the presence of booby-traps. [Royal Scots]

varied widely between units. The last-known specification is UK/ISC/C4044, of 27 April 1967 – for the Royal Navy.

No. 5 Dress trousers lasted longer than the blouse – during the winter of 1970 large quantities of battledress trousers and some blouses were issued to troops in Northern Ireland for wearing under the DPM camouflaged suit.

Limited Wars

The bitter winters experienced by British troops during the Korean War (1950–3) finally convinced the Army that battledress was inadequate as a fighting uniform. The troops in Korea at first wore JG in the summer and battledress in the winter months, but the winters were so harsh that battledress had to be supplemented by fur-lined caps with ear flaps and various items of warm clothing, usually obtained from the US Army. At home, development of a new combat dress was pursued urgently.

In the later stages of the Korean War, new combat dress was issued. This was made from a water-repellent, windproof gaberdine of a grey-green colour not dissimilar to OD. Answering one of the major criticisms of battledress, the new blouse had an all-round skirt and draw-strings at waist and thigh to protect against wind, and the trousers were closed around the ankles with gaiters or more popularly with short puttees. The jacket had several inner and outer pockets, with zip and button fastenings. The trousers had pockets similar to battledress. For additional protection, a parka was issued. This had a synthetic fur lining and a hood. Ammo boots were ditched in favour of new boots with thick moulded rubber soles.

During the 1950s, the definition of temperate areas was the United Kingdom and north-west Europe including BAOR, Canada and the USA. Semi-tropical areas were Gibraltar, Cyprus, Malta, Egypt, Hong Kong, Japan and Korea. Tropical areas were East Africa, Aden and Red Sea ports, West Africa, Sudan, Burma, Carribbean, Iraq, the Persian Gulf, Ceylon, India, Malaya and New Guinea.

In Canada, the USA and all semi-tropical and tropical areas, KD was prescribed for all duties, except that Green Drill was to be worn for operations in Hong Kong, Japan and Korea, Ceylon, India, Malaya and New Guinea. Tropical kit was issued on a scale of three bush jackets, three tropical shirts, three (later two) pairs of drill trousers, three pairs of drill shorts, three pairs of stockings, two pairs of hosetops and, in some areas, one slouch hat; officers were issued with three pairs of worsted slip-on rank badges.

During the 1950s there were developments in equipment, waterproof battle-suits, clothing to withstand arctic conditions (aided by experience in Korea), caps (similar to those worn by men of the Afrika Korps), body armour and NBC protection.

Combat Dress

Once National Service ended, the new all-volunteer, all-Regular Army wanted to escape from battledress which was never exactly smart for parade and not really popular for fighting. The authorities wanted the soldiers to look smart, military and comfortable, so decided to issue two sets of clothing per man, one for parade and one for combat and training. For 'best', the blue No. 1 Dress had been designed but this fell into disrepute as it looked like a station porter's uniform, so a khaki uniform based on officers' service dress was devised, which became No. 2 Dress. For the fighting dress, clothing was developed based on that issued in Korea. This combat clothing began to be issued generally for operations and training in all temperate climates.

In the mid-1960s, soldiers' dress was rationalized and the first officers' dress regulations to be published since 1934 were issued in 1969 which, with amendments, have remained in force until today. The variations in dress were codified into twelve orders: battledress was included as the fifth order of dress, but the new temperate fighting dress was No. 8 and the new warm-weather fighting dress, although not available, was already listed as No. 9. In 1971, the list was expanded into fourteen orders (battledress was listed, but as obsolete). The orders are broken down into temperate and warm-weather; some orders apply only to officers; the orders will not cover all occasions, and officers must use their discretion in what they wear and order their troops to wear; and naturally, there is considerable variation between regiments as to how far they deviate from regulations. What is clear, however, is that Nos. 8 or 9 Dress and No. 2 Dress form the modern British soldier's basic kit, and are the same for all ranks.

The original version of combat dress was plain OG – a greyish-green – and comprised loose trousers and loose, hip-length jacket. This was first issued in 1970. The second pattern of combat dress introduced DPM, and appeared in 1972. There have been several patterns of DPM temperate combat dress since.

No. 8 Dress (Temperate Disruptive Pattern Material [DPM] Combat Uniform [Cold/Wet] is issued on a scale of two suits per man for field wear in temperate areas by soldiers and officers. According to regulations: 'Combat dress is a personal issue, not covered by clothing allowance, and is issued for wear in temperate and semi-tropical areas only. It will be withdrawn from the soldier on posting to tropical areas and will be re-issued as part-worn.' The assembly consists of 'boots, DMS, soldier pattern' (or special pattern as authorized, such as General Issue for use on public duties); DPM combat smock and liner; DPM lined combat trousers; 'combat drawers, pyjama' for cold weather; heavy wool jersey (part of the combat assembly); head-dress (combat cap, combat hood, or beret or bonnet TOS, or DPM-covered steel helmet), but head-dress embellishments (hackles and plumes) are not supposed to be issued.

A tropical DPM took longer to develop. No. 9 Dress (Tropical Disruptive Pattern Material Combat Uniform [Jungle/Desert]) was introduced in 1976. It is a version of No. 8 Dress in a lightweight DPM. This replaced khaki drill and dark green uniform in overseas stations. It consists of DPM hat, DPM tropical jacket and trousers, and boots DMS. Three suits per man are issued for field wear in warm-weather areas – Brunei, Canada (summer), Carribbean, Hong Kong, Mediterranean, Nepal and the United States. In some overseas stations, both Nos. 8 and 9 Dress may be worn in appropriate seasons and at certain hours of the day, at the discretion of the C. in C. or GOC. in C.

There are special combat smocks for parachutists and the SAS. A DPM waterproof smock and trousers are also issued. Various overclothes are issued, notably a white snow smock for camouflage in the Arctic, and particularly NBC suits which are worn over DPMs.

In 1966, the decision was affirmed that rank badges on combats would not be coloured, but would be of plain khaki worsted. Badges and chevrons are embroidered in khaki or dark brown on an OD background and on the DPM smock are worn on the right arm by ORs and on epaulette slides by officers. According to regulations: 'The heavy wool jersey is issued without shoulder-straps. Officers may wear shoulder-straps on the jersey as an optional item to be provided at individual expense.' Plain khaki badges of rank are worn on it, too.

The original intention was that no badges were to be worn on DPMs, except the Army flying badge (parachutist's wings) and air despatch crews' worsted skill-at-arms badges worn by qualified personnel when on strength with airborne formations but not when with other formations. Subsequently, 5 Airborne Brigade (DZ) arm flashes, UDR slip-on flashes and the Berlin Brigade formation sign are the only other badges permitted on Nos. 8 and 9 Dress.

Shirt-sleeve order was also worn with combat dress trousers. Officially only KF shirts (later-pattern green rather than khaki) are to be worn, but officer pattern shirts are also worn, and No. 2 dress shirts unofficially. With rolled sleeves, WOs' rank badges are worn on a green cotton wrist band; some have metal badges, and others cloth. Combat dress jackets are often worn officially or otherwise as inclement weather clothing with barrack dress, with either barrack dress or lightweight trousers and over No. 2 Dress. This became very common after issues of the Army raincoat ceased.

For all ranks, berets, or 'Bonnet, Khaki, TOS' for Scottish infantry regiments, or the Irish Bonnet for Irish infantry, are worn with Nos. 8 and 9 Dress, unless steel helmets are ordered. A peaked DPM cap and a hood are also issued.

The regulation colour for berets is dark blue, with numerous exceptions. The Rifles, Queen's Royal Irish Hussars, Light Division, Gurkha Rifles, Small Arms School, WRAC and UDR have rifle green. The Light Infantry have dark green. Scots Dragoon Guards and QARANC wear grey berets. The Guards Division, Foot Guards, the Royal Anglians (since 1976) and Royal Pioneers have khaki berets. RMP and WRAC Provost wear scarlet. The Parachute Regiment have maroon, the SAS Regiment tan, the AAC light blue, and other

Airborne formations have maroon. The Intelligence Corps wear cypress green, Royal Hussars chocolate brown and the RTR black. The Royal Marines and RA Commando forces wear No. 8 Dress with the green beret. Badges are worn on coloured cloth backings on berets by several formations.

The beret colours are generally regimental. For instance, the regiments comprising the King's Division wear different colours. The Duke of Wellington's wear brown, the Queen's Lancashire and 1 King's wear navy-blue; the RIR wear a green caubeen, not beret; and the Green Howards, Prince of Wales's Yorkshire and 1 King's Own Borderers wear the same brown beret but with different flashes.

Several beret colours came about as 'private ventures' during the Second World War. For instance, the 60th and Rifles Brigades, proud of their rifles origins, began to wear a rifle-green or very dark green patch behind their beret badges, and then began to wear berets of the same colour – a deeper, richer shade than the Commandos. After the war, as their HQ was around the corner from the Palace, their OC asked HM The King if he liked their beret colour, and he said that he did, so the OC promptly told the Army Council he had Royal Approval. When the Light Infantry and Royal Green Jackets amalgamated, the rifle-green colour was retained.

Regulations state that regimental plumes and hackles worn by Scottish and Irish infantry and other Fusiliers should not be worn on bonnets or berets in No. 8 Dress Order. This is frequently flouted.

Initially, No. 8 Dress was worn with 'Boots, DMS, combat, ankle, soldier pattern' and short gaiter puttees (Fox's pattern or as issued). From 1982, 'Boots, combat, high' were issued. These have a high, protective flexible calf, and so gaiters were discarded. They are worn with issue, or privately purchased Gometex waterproof socks.

Footcare is a basic part of soldiering. 'Spit and polish' may have diminished, but the happy soldier still attends to his footwear carefully. When DMS boots first arrive, they have chroming on them which has to be removed. To do this, heat the handle of a metal spoon or the spike of an Army spike knife and 'iron off' the chroming. Then the boot can be highly polished. To polish DMS boots, take a wet duster and a tiny bit of polish at a time until they shine – but there is no 'bulling' in the Army of the 1990s as this ruins the waterproof qualities of combat boots high. To keep combat boots high waterproof use neatsfoot oil as used on saddles (or Mazola cooking oil) – but if too much neatsfoot is used and the temperature drops below zero, the oil freezes and leads to frostbite. Sensible men take hammers and beat their boots to soften them before first wearing them. Hard regiments are alleged to chew the tops of the uppers.

7. Officers and sergeants of the Berlin Detachment, 13/18th Royal Hussars (QM) pose in July 1946. Naturally, it had been the Guards who had started the sartorial modification of battledress to take in the fullness of the blouse to look smarter on parade, tantamount to authorization, and other regiments followed. During the period battledress was in service, blouses and trousers of contrasting patterns were frequently issued and worn, either in an attempt to use stocks economically or to match the varying shades of khaki to avoid the so-called 'sports jacket and flannels' effect. [13/18th Hussars]

8. Two Women Provosts of the Edinburgh Territorial Army branch seen in typical post-war women's battle-dress and in typical Edinburgh environment. They wear c/w red cover to their forage caps and black arm-bands with red 'MP'. Battle-dress was first issued to women of the Auxiliary Territorial Service (ATS) in 1941, for members of mixed anti-aircraft units, for convoy drivers and ambulance drivers, and later to the ATS overseas, except in India and the tropics. Women's organizations to wear it included QARANC, until 1962, and Mechanized Transport Service, until 1947, when their colour changed to bottle-green. [TA MP via G. Williamson]

9. Privates Trevena and Charlesworth of the WRAC step out in fine military fashion in 1957. They wear women's-pattern battle-dress blouse with neck buttoned, and trousers. The first women's blouse was of 1937 style, with brass four-hole buttons, and 'ivory' buttons on the shoulder-straps, and nickel-plated brass belt buckle. The neck was worn open over a shirt and tie. There were twenty sizes. In late 1942, serge facings, plastic buttons and the 1940 'austerity' features were authorized; there were now only six sizes! A single hook and eye was retained at the collar. The pattern introduced on 16 February 1948 resembled the men's blouse. Women wore either a khaki skirt, or trousers closed by buttons on the left hip, with or without field-dressing and map pockets. [WRAC]

10. National Service gunner on leave 'somewhere in southern England' in the late 1940s. After the grant-ing of permission to ORs to wear open collars and ties which exposed the khaki drill facing of the collar, var-ious deviations were prac-tised: the facing was first sponged when it became spoiled; then scrubbed; then bleached; and finally replaced by a longer lasting, better-looking material. [F. Carno]

11. The members of the Army Physical Training Corps in 1945 went to work in issue track suits which shared several characteristics with the battledress in which the troops they trained went to work and war. [Army Physical Training Corp]

12. All are wearing Battle-dress, but these seven Royal Scots in Palestine in 1946 show the wide variations in patterns and various treatments of open collars worn by the British Army in the late 1940s. The man third from the right has the latest pattern. To avoid a rumpled look, weights – often strung on lavatory chain – and later elastic rings were worn round the inside trouser leg to hold it down over the anklet, as shown by the man second left. The first issue ties were cheaply made of sand drill, and were unpopular. Soldiers bought their own ties, like officers, which annoyed the authorities, but the issue of woven ties solved the problem. [Royal Scots]

13. A Royal Scots trooper in Palestine during 1948, wearing his divisional sign on his left shoulder and what appears to be a Glengarry unconventionally with its centre pushed forward into a peak as a sun-guard. [Royal Scots]

14. Demob time: three members of the Argyll and Sutherland Highlanders in a tented camp in Lydda, Palestine, in 1948. The war, mosquitoes and gas had combined to eliminate the Highlanders' kilt irrevocably as active service or training dress. They wear KD shirts and shorts, and 1938-pattern equipment with back packs and belt-order packs. [A&SH]

15. On the Rhine, on exercise with BAOR HQ on 9 July 1949, an Argyll and Sutherland Highlander soaked with sweat with the look of resigned desperation familiar on the faces of company radio operators, a man who really has to work hard. He wears a collared 'shirt, KF', TOS and 1938-pattern equipment. He has his radio in a pack and is wearing pouches. With the advent of ties, the collarless khaki flannel (KF) shirts were phased out and replaced by other patterns until the issue of a standardized pattern in 1950. Lend-Lease US Army khaki shirts were also issued – some surviving into the 1970s and still much sought after! [A&SH/BAOR]

16. Royal Scots arrive in Berlin for field service in about 1955 in Marching Order plus kitbag, with comment clear on their faces. The pattern of greatcoat introduced with battledress in 1938 was similar to the officers' greatcoat. All had pleated backs held in by a half-belt which could be unbuttoned to let the coat be worn over equipment, but this was unusual. [Royal Scots]

15

16

17. Royal Scots leaving Berlin No. 18 in about 1955, with further clear body-language comment. They wear late-pattern battle-dress and well-blancoed 1937 webbing – the standard British personal equipment, the great stocks of which, produced for the wartime Army, were used to equip the bulk of the Army for nearly two decades post-1945. Cold War troops and those who fought Britain's minor Middle Eastern wars wore it; those who fought most of Britain's other wars during the period wore 1944 equipment. [Royal Scots]

18. A long trudge in the snow for Argyll and Sutherland Highlanders with a platoon weapon in Berlin during the winter of 1955. It is clear how the 2ic IO got the job: he's got the jeep. Battledress did not give adequate protection against the cold, even with woollen underwear and gloves. For

19

20

cold weather, khaki woollen gloves were issued (Gurkhas alone had dark green). [A&SH]

19. Argyll and Sutherland Highlanders load a heavy machine-gun (sustained fire-support weapon), boxed .303in link ammunition and equipment on to a truck in Berlin's winter of 1955. The man at the right carries the Vickers; the man second right carries the dial sight in a box and the cleaning rod; the man behind him has the aiming post. The man at the right has the short bayonet and the '08/'37-pattern felt-covered enamelled sheet steel bottle on his web belt, and a Mark IV SMLE. [A&SH]

20. Middlesex Regiment, old and new. Old wears 1878-pattern helmet; new is in Fighting Order but, bulled-up as though he were on parade, wears 'best' battledress. Both wear ammo boots, worn with gaiters on battledress. Soldiers spent hours creating the obligatory mirror-like gloss on the toe-caps and heels of their best pair of ammunition boots. Some regiments demanded that the brass lace eyelets be shone with metal polish. 'Ammunition' was derived from 'munition' which was applied to all military stores and equipment, not merely to projectiles and explosives. Many articles from public stores which were issued to soldiers received the prefix of 'Ammunition', such as 'ammunition loaf', with the idea of indicating the source of issue. [Middlesex Regiment]

21. Troops of 5th Battalion, The Buffs, listen to their officer before a brigade skill-at-arms competition, believed to be in Norfolk in 1965. The 1st and 2nd Battalions, The Buffs, were Regulars, and the 5th was TA, and so at this late date continue to wear No. 5 Dress – battledress, with which the TA continued to be issued for several years after the Regular Army. They wear the new-style helmet – note the spider, crown, net and chinstrap. This looks like a Section Match, fired with two LMGs and six riflemen and commencing at 600 yards, LMGs and rifles moving independently, coming down to 300 yards to simulate fire and movement. [Canterbury Museums, 5th Bn, The Buffs]

22. Troops of 5th Battalion, The Buffs, about to take part in the brigade skill-at-arms competition, wearing battledress and berets. Two men wear zipper-fronted smocks. One-piece berets with a leather-covered rim – worn in black by RTR since 1924 – were introduced for some categories of troops early in the Second World War, in different colours. For the rest of the army, a khaki beret – worn in North Africa in 1942 by motor rifle battalions – became issue, ousting the detesting GS cap. It was replaced by a midnight-blue beret in the late 1940s but the Foot Guards kept khaki; the SAS had adopted and kept sand, the Light Infantry green, the Paras maroon, the AAC sky-blue, the Royal Hussars chocolate, the Intelligence Corps cypress and RTR black. [Canterbury Museums, 5th Bn, The Buffs]

23. Two members of the 7th RTR in Korea with their Churchill tank, brewing up. The bending man is wearing the now-famous 'jersey, wool, heavy', first issued during the Korean War. The corporal wears black beret, and battledress with woolly-pully under it. The ubiquitous woolly-pully can be traced to those heavy khaki pullovers issued in Korea, and worn with pride by veterans. [Tank Museum]

24

24. The 1st Battalion, Middlesex Regiment, on service in Korea in 1951. It is very cold. The man at the left wears a balaclava and mitts. Troops arrived in Korea with battledress and windproof suits against the cold. Woollen serge, as a material for field uniform, had been seen to be obsolete when the US Army introduced its 'layered' concept of combat clothing in 1943. The British followed the lead, introducing their own 'Combat Dress' as a winter uniform during the Korean War. [Middlesex Regt]

25. Men of a Durham Light Infantry night patrol in Korea, 1953. Left to right: Privates Joseph Walton and Roy Reay and Lance-Corporal John Morgan. They are wearing the new gaberdine combat suit (fitting like

25

denim overalls) and woolly-pullies. They wear cap-comforters, a simple tube of stretchy woollen material, an effective piece of kit still on issue. They have lots of automatic weapons, suggesting a snap ambush. Morgan has a bayonet on his weapon, handy for searching. Reay's magazines are too long to fit in his pouches so he has them in his top pockets. Walton has a Bren Mk 3 LMG (30-round box magazine). Behind them is another Bren held by 'finger-less mitts'. [Durham LI]

26. 'C' Company, Argyll and Sutherland Highlanders at work with LMGs in the sitting position on the field firing range of the Divisional Battle School, Sai Kung, on 29 April 1952. The men are in pairs: a gunner and a No. 2 who is an instructor. They wear a mix of JG and KD dress – permitted in this area by Regulation. The variety of headgear is interesting – the gunners wear bush hats; of the No. 2s, two at left are wearing an 'Afrika Korps' cap and a beret, and the nearest is wearing a Glengarry for, being instructors, they wear regimental or Corps head-dress. They are wearing 1944-pattern webbing, as can be seen from the double braces. [A&SH]

27. Wearing jungle-green, a trooper with an SLR of the

Argyll and Sutherland Highlanders, Singapore, 1950s. JG rapidly became blackened with sweat. He is wearing high-leg jungle boots and jungle hat, 1944-pattern webbing and carries a bandolier for clips of five rounds. Post-war, stocks of the 1944 equipment were used as originally intended for campaigning in the East – though not always in the jungle that inspired it, because after it became general issue in Malaya, it was later issued in Korea, Kenya and the Persian Gulf as well as Borneo. [A&SH]

BATTLEDRESS PATTERNS

Battledress, Serge, 1937 Pattern. The original pattern, the 1937-pattern, authorized in 1938 for all arms except horsed, was issued in April 1939 to equip the influx of militia National Servicemen. The waist-length, single-breasted blouse was made of a rough serge with stand-and-fall collar, fly front, pleated breast patch pockets with flap and concealed buttons, plus inner pockets. At the waist the blouse was gathered into a waistband and fastened with a tab to a flat metal buckle on the right of centre. It had pleats at the base of the sleeve. The trousers were straight, and generously fitting with, in addition to normal back and hip pockets, an awkwardly placed large patch pocket with a flap on the left, front thigh just where a crease should be, and a sealed pleated pocket (containing a field dressing) on the right front just below the waist. There were four belt loops long enough to accommodate the 1937-pattern webbing belt. The loops buttoned at the upper ends. At the bottoms the trousers had a tab and button, so that they could be fastened around the ankle for wear with black leather ankle boots and web anklets. All buttons on the original pattern were pressed brass with four holes, except those on the shoulder-straps and field dressing pocket. (Some buttons were made of vegetable compound and were green; later buttons were four-holed plastic.)

The cloth specified for the 1938 pattern was Serge No. 1 55 inch Pattern No. T 90. The inside edges of the front of the blouse, two deep inside pockets, blouse belt lining and trouser pockets were of a light sandy-yellow drill material, Drill No. 2 Drab. On each garment was stitched a calico or linen label bearing the contractor's name; the place and date of manufacture; the broad arrow name of the article; the size; and details of measurements.

The shortcomings of battledress were soon apparent. Some were faults in design, others resulted from poor manufacturing and quality control by some factories. Successive alterations were made to it. Instructions were issued to ensure that stressed seams were double-sewn, and buttons were attached more securely. Other regulations altered the position of the pockets to prevent the snagging of webbing equipment. Collars were lined with Drill No. 2 to reduce skin chafing. Trousers were lined with cotton over the lower back for further protection. In 1940, instructions were issued for a slimmer cut to the blouse, so as to use less cloth in line with wartime economies. In 1941, the straps for gathering the gaiters were deleted. The concealed buttons and pocket pleats of the first pattern did not in fact disappear in 1940, although battledress suits without them are referred to as '1940 Pattern'.

Battledress, Serge, 1940 Pattern. A full new pattern of battledress was devised in 1940, termed the 'utility' 1940 pattern, although it was not issued until June 1942 and the first to wear it in action were First Army troops in North Africa later that year. The primary consideration in the design of the new issue was economy in material and manufacturing. The fullness of the blouse was reduced, giving it a distinctively close-fit. The fly fastening of the blouse, pockets and cuffs were deleted, leaving all buttons, except on the trouser fly, exposed. Pocket pleats and belt loops disappeared. The blouse was to be attached to the trousers by two buttons instead of three, and there was no

longer a fly to hide them. In response to criticism, however, the trousers were given another back curtain for greater warmth. The 1938 brass buttons were deleted; from July 1942 all buttons were to be four-hole plastic (some officers adopted leather buttons). The cloth specified for the 1940 pattern was Serge No. 1 55 inch, lighter than for the 1938 pattern. The collar, inner edges of the front of the blouse, inside pockets, blouse belt lining and trouser pockets were of Drill No. 2 Drab. Each garment had a calico or linen label. In 1943, one blouse inside breast pocket was deleted. The first battledress blouse buckles were prongless, in brass, but wartime needs forced substitution of pressed metal or thick plated wire buckle types, depending on availability and manufacturer.

Battledress, Women's. The first specification covering 'Blouse, Battledress, Serge, ATS' (Auxiliary Territorial Service) was issued on 4 September 1941, for a garment in the 1937 style; buttons were brass four-hole apart from the 'vegetable ivory' on the shoulder-straps, and the waist belt buckle was a toothed, nickel-plated brass type. In late 1942, serge facings were authorized as the neck was worn open over a shirt and tie, and at the same time the austerity features of the 1940 pattern were introduced, and all buttons became plastic. One hook and eye was retained at the collar. This pattern remained in force until 16 February 1948. The later pattern resembled the male blouse. The battledress blouse was worn with either a khaki shirt, or trousers closed by buttons on the left hip, with or without field dressing and map pockets.

Battle Dress, Olive Drab, WA (War Aid). War material production programmes called for US factories to produce Battle Dress for British soldiers – the US used two words. The main recognition feature of the US blouse was that the fly front over the buttons was retained, but the pockets and cuffs had exposed buttons. The trousers also retained the belt loops of the British first pattern. US material and manufacture were superior to British. Battle Dress, OD, WA, was manufactured in the USA from about 1943 and shipped to the Middle East for issue to British and Commonwealth forces and for partisans. It was worn almost exclusively in this theatre.

Battledress, Serge, Canadian Pattern. A much coveted pattern of battledress was that manufactured in Canada which, styled after the British 1937 pattern, was superior in materials and manufacture. The cut was more generous. The cloth was much finer, smoother, a wool-filled, bronze-green serge very different from the lighter, duller khaki serge of British suits. Pleats were always provided in Canadian (and Australian) battledress as they remained fuller cut than British-made battledress (the 1938 pattern had pleats at the base of the sleeve but later British patterns were made plain, though there were exceptions).

Battledress, 1946 Pattern. In 1946, a new pattern blouse was authorized in an attempt to regularize the wear of the garment following permission being granted to ORs to wear ties off-duty and when walking out, but still to wear battledress fastened at the neck on duty. Thus, it retained the stand-up collar but the collar was 'faced' so that it could be worn open. The double hook-and-eye method of closure was discarded in favour of a less obtrusive tab on the left

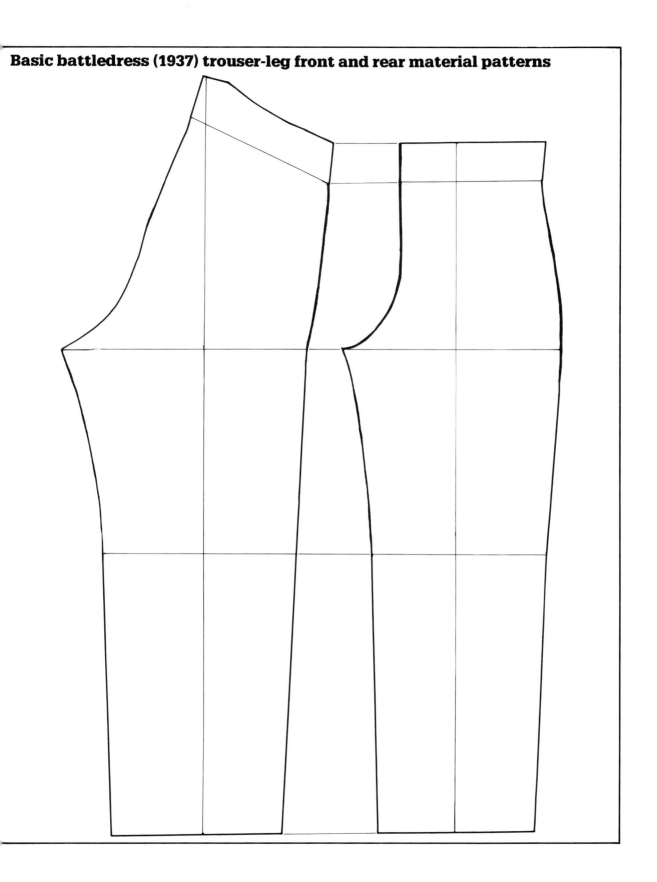

Basic battledress (1937) trouser-leg front and rear material patterns

which could be buttoned on the right so that the collar could be closed, or button-backed on the left to conceal it under the left collar while the collar was worn open, following the Canadian pattern button-back tab. With wartime austerity relaxed, the fly front covering the front buttons and the box-pleated pockets of the original 1937 pattern battledress were re-introduced, and better quality Serge SD (Service Dress) No. 4 56 inch body cloth was introduced. The pocket flaps, the cuffs and the two waist-band buttons for attaching the trousers were still of the button-through type. The 1946 pattern trousers were similar to the 1942 modification of the 1940 pattern, but with an additional six braces buttons.

Battledress Blouse, 1947 Pattern. In 1947, a modified blouse with a 'shirt-type' collar was authorized (Specification UK/CIC/1843, 28 October 1947), inspired by the collar of the US 'Ike' jacket, though the result resembled the German Army's 1944 blouse collar. Closed, it resembled the stand-up collars of previous patterns; opened, it pressed back smoothly in two stepped lapels. Sleeves were of a fuller cut, and the cuff-band pleats of the 1937 pattern were re-introduced.

Battledress, 1949 pattern. The final pattern of British Battledress blouse was similar to the 1947 pattern, but the lapels were smaller, neater and more practical. It appeared in consequence of the new regulation that ties were to be worn by all ranks, on and off duty. The collar was a stepped lapel with a buttonhole on the left; it could not be closed. Officially, a tie was to be worn in the field, which was not comfortable when in the prone firing position. In practice, in the field, the camouflage net face veil was worn as a cravat at the neck of the blouse, rather than a tie. The blouse had two inside breast pockets, like the 1937 pattern. There was a hanger tape at the nape. In 1954, three buttonholes on the waist band superseded two. The trousers were entirely different from previous patterns. They had waist tabs, slanted pockets, two hip pockets and a side-mounted map pocket; the first pattern had had four belt loops buttoned at the top; ten years on, the 1948 pattern re-introduced three loops (4in long, 1in wide) buttoned at the bottom for a web belt. The 1949 pattern battledress remained the standard temperate climate field uniform of the British Army until re-placed by combat dress. It came to be known as 'No. 5 Dress' in a range of fourteen Orders of Dress in the British Army. The last British Army battledress amendments were issued in June 1954.

28

28. Jungle Platoon of 'D' Company, Argyll and Sutherland Highlanders, Singapore, on patrol in the jungle. Their socks have been pulled out of their boots and up over their trousers. During the 1950s, troops found the 1944 pattern had serious drawbacks when packing the operational loads then required — light on ammunition, heavy on rations. Webbing rotted quickly. Metal fittings broke. Necessity forced troops to modify packs with padded shoulder-straps, to use parachute rigging to secure kit and make repairs, and even to use para-drop webbing to make new belts to which were fitted locally made canvas pouches, native knives and issue water-bottles. Australian-pattern sleeping-bags were used. This patrol, however, is travelling very light. [A&SH]

1949 pattern battledress trousers

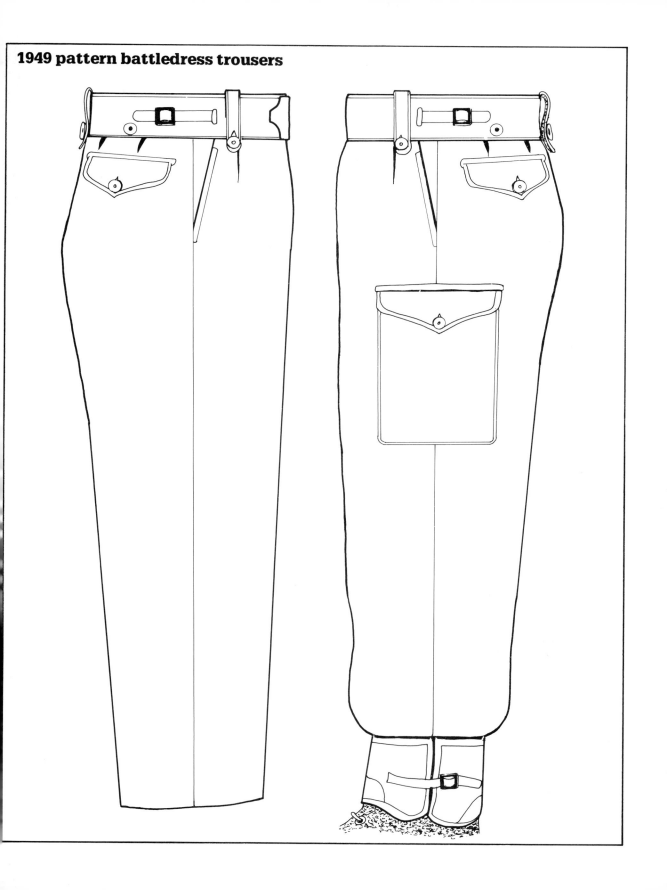

1946 pattern battledress blouse; and faced collar buttoned up

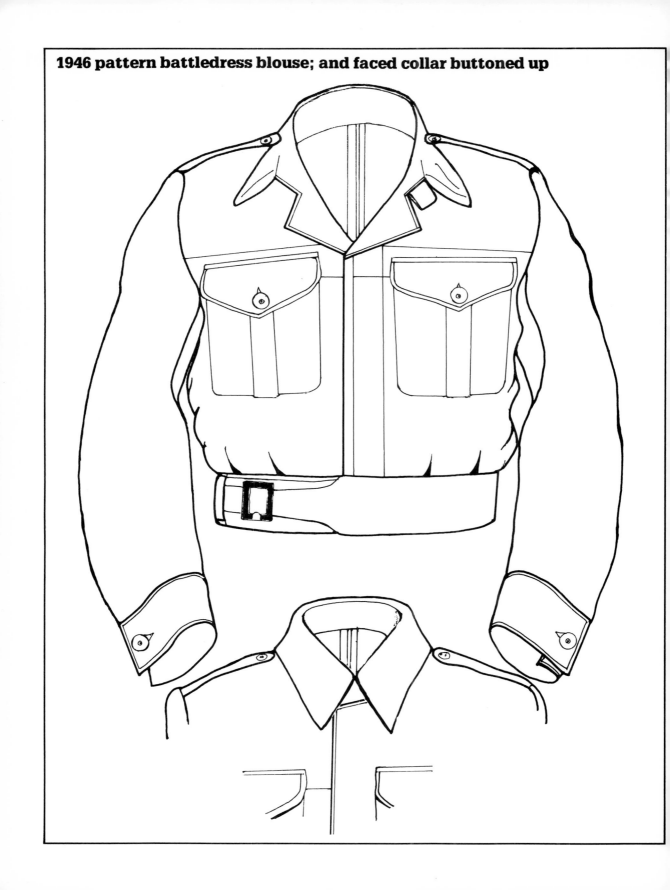

1947 pattern battledress blouse

29. Iban tracker with the Argyll and Sutherland Highlanders in Singapore during the 1950s wearing standard British-issue jungle gear. He has a band round the bottom of his slacks to keep out insects. [A&SH]

30. A 1951 National Service Recruits Light Infantry Brigade Group pass out at the KSLI Depot, Copthorne Barracks, Shrewsbury, before posting to their regiment. Left to right: P. C. Goulding, W. R. G. Hank, D. N. Sargent, D. G. Hill, K. Pidgeon, A. Mottershead, W. T. R.?, and R. E. Bowen. They wear midnight-blue berets and the smart 1949-pattern battledress showing the restrained lapels. The shoulder-titles are light infantry, but cap badges are the old Oxford and Bucks pattern worn by recruits to the Light Infantry Brigade Group. During the war, the cloth used for British battledress varied considerably in weight and colour, depending on the batch from the mill, and a parade seldom looked uniform, even a single man varying in shade, finish and weight! Now, using Serge SD No. 4 56-inch cloth, an even appearance results. [KSLI, via G. Archer Parfitt]

31. During the early 1960s, a soldier of the Argyll and Sutherland Highlanders is instructed by a sergeant weapons instructor on the weapons range in the use of the Energa round. One round is loaded into his rifle, another waits in front of his pit. There is a pouch issued for 1958-pattern equipment which was specifically designed as the Energa pouch. The bayonet frog can be seen clearly on the pouch. The trainee wears denim fatigues over his battledress, 1958-pattern equipment in skill-at-arms order and the new-style helmet. The instructor wears 1940-pattern battledress. [A&SH RHQ]

31

32. During 1959, a member of the 4th Battalion, KSLI (TA) undergoes field training in camp in the use of the 3.5in rocket-launcher. The instructor's nicely creased battledress trousers and woolly-pully are notable. The young soldier wears 1958 webbing skill-at-arms order, his bayonet in a separate frog, and a cape carrier. [KSLI, via G. Archer Parfitt]

32

33. Members of the Middlesex Regiment take it easy in sand dunes on the Essex coast. They have an SLR, SMG and LMG and wear ammo boots with gaiters, lightweight OG trousers, KF shirt and bush hat, with 1938 equipment. [Middlesex Regt]

34. At this KSLI Pay Parade at Copthorne Barracks, Shrewsbury, during 1958, the man being paid wears 1949-pattern battledress. He wears his belt over his blouse waist because – although three belt loops for the web belt were revived on the 1949-pattern battledress, buttoned at the lower ends, one at the seat seam and the other two over the pleats nearest the side pockets (the original pattern trousers had four loops, buttoned at the upper ends) – the belt loops were only used in shirt-sleeve order. The trousers could be worn with or without braces. [KSLI, via G. Archer Parfitt]

35. Members of the Royal Ulster Rifles model their dress orders as in the 1950s, photographed at the RUR Regimental Depot, Ballymena in 1959. In 1945, 1 RUR gave up their red berets on leaving 6 (Airborne) Division while 2 RUR, then in 3 Division, wore their khaki berets pulled down over their left ear like RIR. In 1948, 1 and 2 RUR amalgamated and became 1 RUR (83rd and 86th) and khaki berets were worn pulled down, like the rest of the Army, over the right ear. Later, 1 RUR changed to green caubeens and later still adopted the black hackle above the badge. From 1945 to 1968 these formations wore battledress, KD, tropical kit, winter warfare kit in Korea, No. 2 Dress, woolly-pullies, shorts and anklets, shorts and puttees, stable belts, plastic belts, etc. In 1968, RUR amalgamated with the two other Irish infantry regiments to form The Royal Irish Rangers. [RIR]

36. 'Beatnik' Hazelwood of 'B' Battalion, 1st Regiment, Royal Horse Artillery, models the practical brown overalls worn by self-propelled gun crews in 1960. The denims were based upon the battledress pattern, but were one-piece. [A. Prewer]

37. A very smart Centurion tank crew of the RTR, stationed in Hong Kong in 1960, await inspection. Hong Kong was designated semitropical, and KD was issued for normal wear with JG for active service. The crew wear their 'best' battledress (1949 model) with 1944-pattern equipment, an interesting combination. The 1949-pattern trousers had set forward side pockets, two hip pockets with flaps, a thigh pocket with flap on the left outside (no longer front) leg and there was no field-dressing pocket. Worn either with or without braces, they had a waistband, four unseen pleats at front and two at back, three belt loops buttoned at the lower end, two hip straps and buckles, and plain bottoms. [Tank Museum]

38. Members of the Inniskilling Dragoon Guards re-ammunition their Centurion, 'Cool' in 1964. The man on the tank wears battledress. The others wear tankers' overalls. [Tank Museum]

39. A Centurion crew of the Royal Armoured Regiment undertaking arctic clothing trials in the early 1960s. They are wearing 'Cold Weather Warfare' boots with special thick soles and thermal insoles, and an experimental one-piece cold suit. There was much experimentation after the Korean experience. In the 1960s, a soldier in northwest Europe would have a 1960-pattern parka – with the seat panel under the crutch, sewn at the back and fastened to two buttons over the garment's front. [Tank Museum]

40. Members of the Shropshire Yeomanry, 3rd Carabiniers, on exercise in 1962 have ambushed a scout car. For cold weather, they wear Canadian-pattern combat jacket and trousers in OG, similar to Korean War issue, one of a variety of garments seen at this time. [KSLI, via G. Archer Parfitt]

41. A photograph of the Shropshire Yeomanry Team in the 1963 Cumbrian March Competition having their ammo boots inspected before setting off. They wear rain/windproof smocks. Clothing was in transition at this juncture. [KSLI, via G. Archer Parfitt]

42. '1157 Issue': what the well-dressed combatant was issued with in the 1950s, this set belonging to an NCO of the Middlesex Regiment. 'AF1157' is the soldier's personal kit record. [Middlesex Regt]

43. A member of the 1950s Middlesex Regiment models an NBC suit Mark I. The patches of flocky material at the knees, elbows and forearms protect the soldier while crawling or ground firing. He wears crude one-sized mittens now replaced by inner cotton and outer rubberized gloves, both sized. He does not wear overboots which are now issued but are generally considered to be useless for moving and fighting. [Middlesex Regt]

44. Wearing tropical gear, 'B' Company Tracker Team of the Argyll and Sutherland Highlanders, Singapore, *c.* 1964–6. On the ground in front of them is a GS carrier with, on top of it, an ancillary bag. The man at the right in the rear row wears a bandolier of clips of 5×7.62in ball ammunition, as do two others. [A&SH]

45

45. Light machine-gun number of the Argyll and Sutherland Highlanders, Singapore (HQ Far East Land Forces), February 1964. His machine-gun has a ladder sight (by his right forearm), a thirty-round box magazine and bipod legs folded under the front strop; note the gas regulator just in front of the bipod's swivel point. He wears 1944 webbing. Many soldiers modified the 1944 pattern; the first modification was moving the ammo pouches from their original position — as can be seen here, it was obstructive especially for LMG — to one similar to that of the 1958-pattern pouches. Some '44 pouches had fittings for this purpose, but most had to be modified. [A&SH]

46

46. An RAVC Specialist Dog Handler on patrol with a Tracker during the Malayan Campaign, with his Labrador Tracker Dog. The soldier wears bush hat and OG shirt. Clipped to his belt is the harness and pilot line used when the dog is being worked. He is armed with the Sterling SMG and has a 1944-pattern canvas pack, while the other man has a rucksack. [RAVC]

47. Royal Scots, in a 3in mortar base position near Tripoli in 1963, wearing khaki slacks and – as the regiment permitted – Khaki or OG drill bush jackets of regimental pattern. Regimental Regulations at this date said of the bush jacket: 'Loops fitted for belt of [drill] with two-prong brass buckle. Brass badges of rank. Silver RS Titles on shoulder-straps. No collar badges. Anodized small buttons (with split rings).' [Royal Scots]

48. With their white-painted Ferret scout car and their blue berets, these Troopers of 4/7th Royal Dragoon Guards were serving with the United Nations Forces in Cyprus. They are cleaning their weapons before a patrol round Nicosia airport. Ian Knipe (left) strips his SMG, Anthony Middleton holds a 30 Browning, while Brian Hancock (right) uses the service flanellete '4×2' to clean his weapon. [4/7th Dragoon Guards]

49. A member of the 5th RTR on patrol in Aden, with the enemy's graffiti behind him. He wears regimental black beret, 1950-pattern khaki drill bush jacket and shorts, dark hose and shoes. He wears belt-order webbing, with one ammo pouch and one waterbottle pouch. He is armed with an L1 SLR. [Tank Museum]

50. Three riflemen of the Argyll and Sutherland Highlanders with an armoured scout car patrol in Aden. They wear belt-order; the man on the right has appropriated an Energa pouch, used for general kit. All three wear glengarry with regimental dicing and badge, khaki slacks, and black DMS ankle boots with short puttees (they could be khaki or olive green); the outer men wear 1950 pattern KD bush jackets, while the middle man wears a Shirley KD short-sleeve order shirt. [A&SH]

51. Members of an Argyll and Sutherland Highlanders patrol in Aden shortly before setting out on a patrol. They wear glengarry, KD bush jacket and slacks, DMS boots and puttees. Second from the right is the Number 1, with the GPMG beside him; on the right is the Number 2, with his Larkspur series radio, just in front of which is a spare battery. On the far left of the photograph is a 2in mortar. The ammunition bandoliers carry 7.62mm link – superseding the Bren Mk 3 ammunition which so far has been illustrated. [A&SH]

PERSONAL EQUIPMENT

1937 Pattern. At about the same time as battledress was introduced, there was a change in load-carrying equipment to meet the needs of all branches of a newly mechanized army. Like the 1908 pattern it was based upon a belt and braces: a 2¼in-wide web belt (dyed khaki) with a patent clasp, and two shoulder braces. Compared to the 1908 pattern, the braces were shaped on the shoulders, the belt was narrower and the fastenings of the small pack were improved so that it could be removed and put on without disturbing the remainder. This was the 1937 pattern. New pouches were fitted which each held two Bren magazines, grenades or smallarms ammunition; a cotton bandolier of fifty rounds was also issued. A new haversack, or small pack was introduced; it was worn on the braces but some units devised a way of wearing it hooked on the pouches without braces. An entrenching tool was carried in a web holder over the buttocks, and the new short bayonet in a frog. The new pattern had one disadvantage – the belt could not be adjusted easily or quickly, which made it difficult to put on a greatcoat. Issues of the 1937 pattern began before the war, replacing all other patterns by mid-war, although by then efforts were being made to replace it in whole or part.

1944 Pattern. Users in Burma found that the 1937 pattern was inadequate for jungle warfare in the Far East so a new pattern of equipment was designed in 1944 for the tough campaign against the Japanese that was foreseen. The design agency took the configuration of the 1937 pattern as their guide, but set out to eliminate the faults reported by users by adopting lighter webbing with alloy metal for the furniture, in order to reduce the weight of the equipment set. Special features in the waist belt and braces theoretically allowed the equipment to be worn comfortably without galling the waist. The US Army eyelet-and-hook method for attaching items to the belt was copied. A canvas rucksack-type pack was issued for use with the 1944 pattern, carried on the shoulder-straps. Pouches and haversack had more volume. The pack interior was partly waterproofed; it had side pockets for the messtin halves and attachments for digging tools and so on. The waterbottle and cup was copied from the excellent US Army canteen. The US design for the poncho was adopted. The webbing was dyed jungle-green. Metal fittings were dulled. The equipment was first issued in 1945 in the Far East.

1958 Pattern. In the 1950s, the War Office initiated development of an equipment set more suitable for mechanized infantry than existing sets. By the late 1950s, a design had emerged which, with minor modification, was issued generally to infantry units in 1960, although it was several years before all units of the Army had the new equipment. This was the 1958 pattern. Its main feature is the yoke, a padded shoulder-harness to distribute weight comfortably and which is attached to a conventional load-bearing waistbelt. The belt carries ammunition pouches, a waterbottle, NBC gear on the sides and a pair of 'kidney pouches' at the rear below which is a poncho-roll. The bayonet is held in loops on the inside face of the left ammunition pouch. The olive drab webbing requires no cleaning or blancoing. The two Orders for wear with the 1958 pattern are designated Combat Equipment, Fighting Order (CEFO), and Combat Equipment, Marching Order (CEMO). In CEFO, a soldier carries what he requires for fighting; when CEMO is ordered, additionally he carries in his field pack what he needs to maintain himself in the field.

CEFO. Ammunition pouches: four full SLR magazines (totalling eighty rounds); one belt (fifty rounds) of GPMG ammunition; two grenades; bayonet and scabbard; weapon cleaning kit.

Kidney Pouches: messtin; combat rations; knife/fork/spoon; washing and shaving kit; footpowder; spare socks; housewife (sewing kit); towel; spare laces.

Attached: poncho in roll; full waterbottle and mug; lightweight pick and shovel; sandbag; respirator and NBC gear.

CEMO. As above plus field pack: beret; cap comforter; drawers; parka; shirt, khaki, flannel; socks; towel; gloves; boot-cleaning kit; PT shoes; boots DMS; sleeping-bag.

1937 pattern web equipment

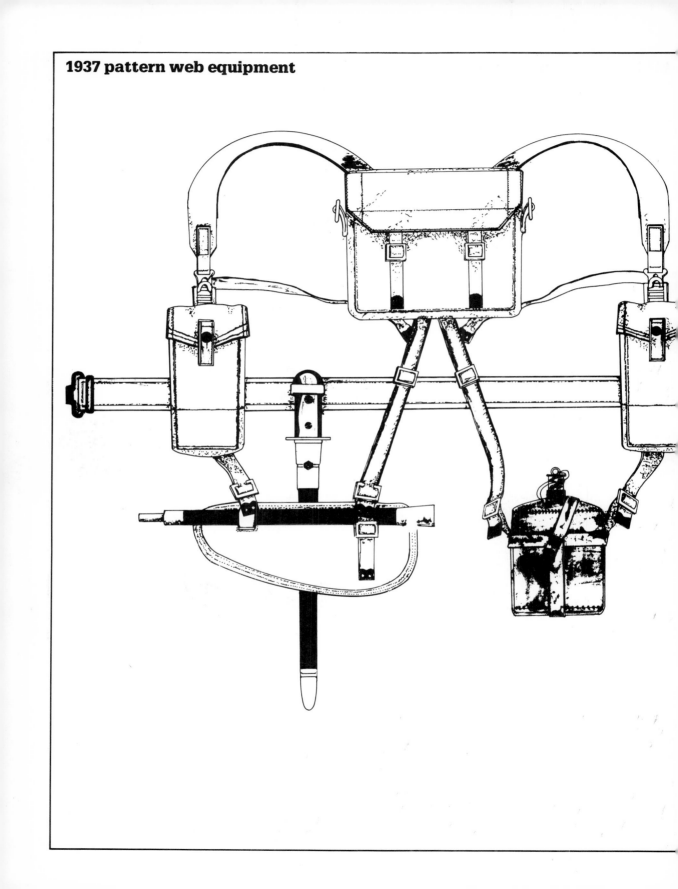

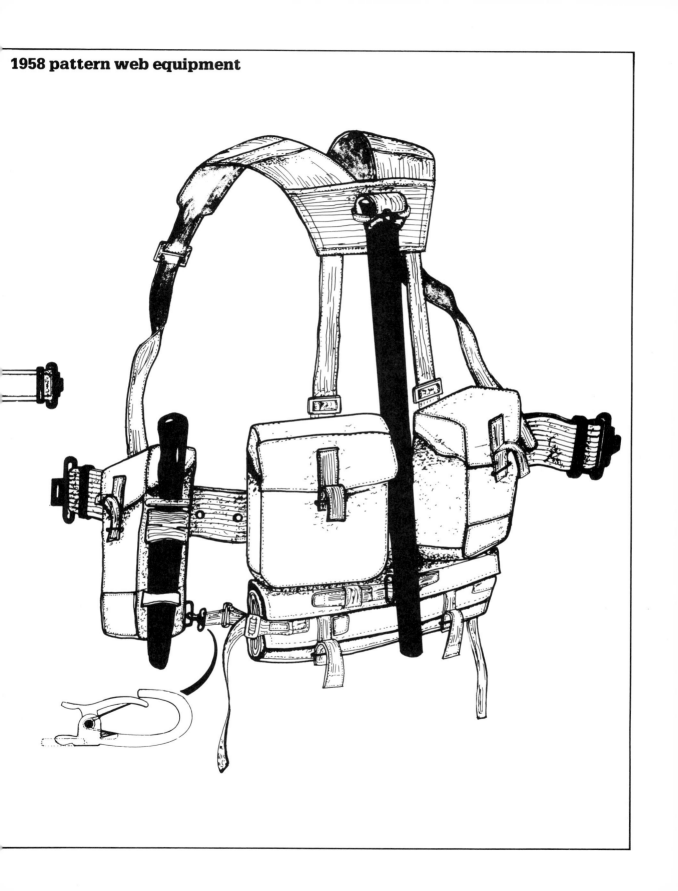

52. 1st Regiment, Royal Horse Artillery, Chestnut Troop, 'B' Sub, at Mukeiros in 1965. Ready-use ammunition is stacked to the left. They wear 1950-pattern KD bush jackets and slacks and 1958 belt, and the dark blue beret. [A. Prewer]

53. WRAC nurses and staff attached to the Argyll and Sutherland Highlanders in Aden, wearing khaki short-sleeve bush jacket and skirt, soft service cap, short hose and shoes. [A&SH]

54. On the Crater Road, Aden, a rifleman of the Argyll and Sutherland Highlanders, wearing 1950 pattern KD bush jacket, with sweat scarf, olive green webbing, 1944-pattern, KD slacks, DMS ankle boots and puttees and with an L1 SLR. The photograph shows the map pocket well. [A&SH]

55. A 2nd lieutenant and sniper of the Argyll and Sutherland Highlanders, somewhere on the Crater, Aden. Snipers work in pairs: a sniper and close protection but the officer here is not the close protection. The sniper has an SMLE No 4 mod. sniper rifle. The officer wears a tropical OG bush jacket; note the epaulettes with 'ASH' badges. Waistband detail is revealed by the sniper. [A&SH]

56. With his SMG to hand, a radio operator of the Argyll and Sutherland Highlanders at rest. He has a G1098 issue watch, and, for a change, he is wearing a khaki bush hat and bound puttees rather than gaiters. [A&SH]

57. In a sangar, Royal Scots clean their weapons after action in the Radfan during 1964. At right, on a GS carrier, is an A41 radio (the battery is the lower section). Behind the men are their personal SLRs; the one at the left has butt number 15. The man at the right is stripping the GPMG; he holds the barrel, while in front of his right left can be seen the top cover. In the foreground are field beds. [Royal Scots]

58. Seen in June 1969, an Argyll and Sutherland Highlanders' Orders Group ('O' Gp) armed with old-pattern, wooden, SLRs, and wearing the cap comforter and the KF Shirt ('shirts hairy'); the leader at the left has had his tailored to fit ('bullshitter'). The photograph shows fine details of attire. [A&SH]

59. Clad in parkas with lined hoods, mittens and over-trousers, Argyll and Sutherland Highlanders on Saracens in the foothills undergo Winter Indoctrination training: 'beautiful but awfa cauld!' [A&SH photo. Ian Christie]

58

59

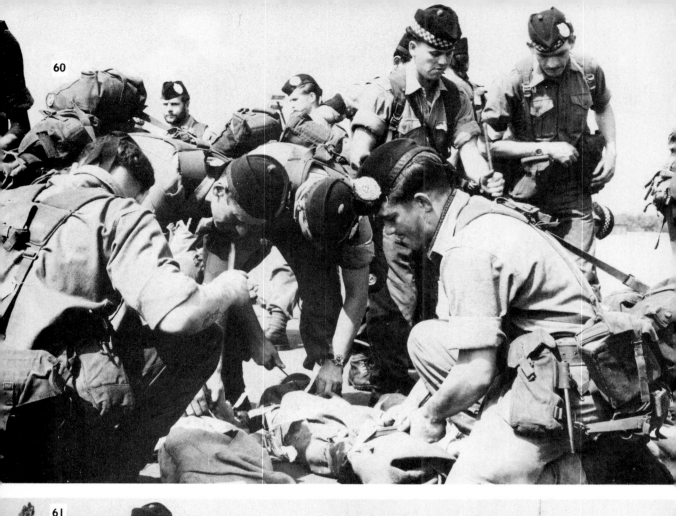

60

61

60. This photograph shows the 1958-pattern webbing very clearly; these Argyll and Sutherland Highlanders open their weapon bundles at Gatow airfield on 26 July 1969, after being airlifted to Berlin in a Britannia of RAF Air Support Command, for a tour in Berlin. When troops travel by air their weapons are wrapped in hessian bundles and stowed in the hold. The man at the right has a luggage label on his webbing and wears a bayonet scabbard but without bayonet – the man second from the right appears to be using his to unpack his kit! The man third from the right is wearing a G1098 issue watch. They have fairly full webbing and all seem to have satchels. [A&SH]

61. The Argyll and Sutherlanders move their weapons at Gatow. They are in shirt-sleeve order (May–October to 18.00 hours) with KF shirt, OG slacks, DMS ankle boots and woollen puttees. The man at the left carries a 1958-pattern sleeping-bag strapped on the top of a large pack. The bearded man is a rarity: an assault pioneer platoon sergeant – the only rank in the British Army entitled to wear a beard. [A&SH]

62. Infantrymen rushing from cover to emplane. They are wearing berets, OG smocks and OG trousers. The spades are carried in the designed position, but they are the wrong way round (their concave, angled shape will dig into the back when the men try to get up from prone firing!); and they should be in a sandbag as the shine from them might attract fatal attention. The 1958 pattern favours the infantryman in an APC or helicopter rather than one on foot in rough terrain. Any equipment design is a com-

promise and the designers saw no need for CEMO to be carried for long periods, so concentrated on producing equipment that would contain fighting loads well, and above which a field pack could be perched for short marches. Men should remove berets when approaching rotors . . . [Westland Helicopters]

63. 'Stick 'em up!' Royal Scots Private Pik Fleming and his Wombat, Osnabrück, 1968. Both men wear familiar kit for exercise in the UK: 1958-pattern webbing, OG trousers with gaiters, DMS boots and khaki flannel shirt with sleeves rolled up. On Fleming's right shoulder-strap can be seen clearly the loop for a strap to go under and, below that, 'D' rings for attaching the large pack. The man at the left helpfully shows off detail of the spade handle attachment on his webbing. [Royal Scots]

64

64. Two members of the Royal Armoured Corps Parachute Squadron in jumping order. [Tank Museum]

65. Royal Scots GPMG gunner and No. 2 on a weapons range in Scotland. They are wearing winter gear. The No. 2 helpfully shows how the 1958-pattern belt can be carried loose. The men wear OG jacket and trousers. [Royal Scots]

66. An FV 432 armoured personnel carrier and four Royal Scots (Corporal McArdle in the foreground) and, in the vehicle, a Gurkha. They are wearing parkas and heavy gloves. [Royal Scots]

67. Corporal John McLoughlan, Argyll and Sutherland Highlanders, on the IS range. He is wearing KF shirt and first-issue DPM combat trousers. Internal Security operations in Ulster have goaded development of protective clothing. New glass-reinforced plastic helmets and leg shields resulted, as did protective vests (nylon and Kevlar) and various kinds of shield. [A&SH]

68. 1st Regiment, Royal Horse Artillery, on training in IS in Northern Ireland during 1969. They have riot shields. In August 1969, the Army's stores contained anti-riot shields, wooden truncheons, pick-axe helves and plastic visors for steel helmets. [A. Prewer]

69. Early days in Belfast: wearing OGs, a private of the Green Howards backed-up by a corporal wearing a steel helmet with visor, conduct door-to-door inquiries. In the early 1970s soldiers in Ulster wore standard 1970-pattern OG trousers, and some wore 1937-pattern webbing gaiters, with woolly-pully and a flak jacket. The visor made a helmet flop down over the face and a lighter combat helmet was swiftly developed. [Green Howards]

70. 1st Battalion, Green Howards in full combat gear prepare for an exercise in Berlin in 1978. They wear the original style DPM jacket, a fine garment whose major drawbacks were that the outer pockets at the front had too little capacity – they were flat sewn, not gussetted – and that if the poplin lining got very wet it took hours to dry out. [Green Howards]

71. 1st Battalion, Green Howards 'bombing-up' with rifle ammunition, Berlin, in 1978. The man on the left has his rounds in his helmet which makes sense, but the man on the right has his scattered about. The only trouble with the left man's method is that he has the old-style helmet and there was so much 'gubbins' inside it that rounds would get lodged up there to your embarrassment later following the declaration of 'No rounds in my possession, sir!' However – in the field the man on the right will not have a nice dry sandbag on which to scatter his rounds! [Green Howards]

72. The Green Howards move off on exercise, Berlin, 1978. [Green Howards]

73. 1st Battalion, Green Howards on a BHE (Battle Hardening Exercise) in Berlin, 1978, showing that foliage camouflage can break up a soldier's outline even in the open! The 1958-pattern webbing does not lend itself easily to attaching camo, and soldiers are encouraged to use bungee, and to sew black elastic hoops on it to keep the foliage on. [Green Howards]

74. Argyll and Sutherland Highlanders wearing DPMs, some with hoods and waterproofs, most with SLRs and two with GPMGs. In the foreground is a Bergen. All the SLRs have SUIT [Sight Unit Individual Trilux]; the SLRs have magazines attached. 'Bisley Bill' – second from right– has an SLR with a GPMG or LSW bipod as used in OPs or on ambush: the rifle is laid on a line of sight, which can thus be held for long periods without effort. [A&SH]

75. A Royal Scots on the rifle range in the kneeling position. He wears Northern Ireland gloves, for IS and FIBUA, which have pads on the backs of the hands and fingers to minimize grazing from 'urban surfaces'. The button-fastening on the DPM cuff can be seen, which is preferred by older soldiers to the velcro in the more recent jackets, as were the previous DPM suits which were more robust but – rumour has it – were too expensive. The soldier wears an Energa pouch – the right-hand ammo pouch has a tube sewn on to it for the round. [Royal Scots]

76. Argyll and Sutherland Highlanders on a route march wearing DPM jacket and lightweight OG trousers combat. The leading man has a hessianed spade across his Bergen-type pack. [A&SH]

77. Argyll and Sutherland Highlanders Lance-Corporals McFarlane and McPherson return to their trenches after a patrol brief-ing during the mid-1980s. They wear boots combat high, lightweight trousers, jackets combat, and helmets combat. They have the old, screw-on BFA. The main point with the BFA is to adjust it to give sufficient blow-back to allow the gun to continue to fire in auto-matic. [A&SH]

78. Private David Pickering of 1st Argyll and Sutherland Highlanders with a light-weight clip-on BFA on the Brecon Beacons in the late 1980s. He is wearing a DPM bush hat. The zipper of his smock can be seen clearly, with a grenade ring on it to pull it up and down. Gren-ade rings come in for a var-iety of equipment uses – such as slings for NBC suit rolls. The diagonal strap is for his respirator satchel. [A&SH]

79. Lance-Corporal Alex Mackenzie of 1st Argyll and Sutherland Highlanders on the Brecon Beacons in 1987. He is wearing standard combat DPM smock and lightweight trousers. At left can be seen the pouch for the first field dressing. Round his neck is a scrim scarf. [A&SH]

80

81

80. Argyll and Sutherlander Corporal Lee's 'B' Company section poses happily in Scottish Lowland Training Area with an MBT and an 84mm anti-tank weapon. They are wearing DPM 'crow caps' (DPM Caps Combat, which are worn when ordered instead of beret, glengarry or helmet). [A&SH]

81. A soldier with a General-Purpose Machine-Gun (GPMG). Clipped to his back straps is his cape carrier ('bum roll') and used to carry his NBC suit. His poncho is bungeed to the pouches. In lacing his boots combat high, he has missed out the top eyelets to relieve the pressure on the top of the calf. The picture shows the limitations of using the GPMG as a light machine-gun! [UKLF]

82. A soldier dressed in full No. 8 Combat Dress carrying a Light Support Weapon (LSW). This is based on the SA80 and has 80 per cent commonality. It has a longer barrel, a bipod for support and a 30-round box magazine. It replaces the GPMG at section level and there are two per section, one in each fire team, providing automatic firepower without encumbrance. [UKLF]

83. A soldier on exercise with the SA80 weapon, wearing a smock, but this is probably a posed photograph. He has scrimmed his DPM helmet which is unusual. He is wearing a KF shirt and a woolly-pully. [UKLF]

84. A unit commander on exercise shows the proper use of DPM helmet for camouflage. He carries a PRC 349 (a commander's unit), and has a single earphone strapped to his head and a throat mike. He is wearing a jacket, foul weather. He has a bayonet fixed. [UKLF]

85. A soldier of 1st Battalion, The Argyll and Sutherland Highlanders, participating in Exercise 'Simex 88' (4–17 June 1988), equipped with his personal laser receivers on his helmet and shoulder. The laser projector is attached to his SA80 rifle. 'Simex' was the longest and most comprehensive exercise held by the British Army in the United Kingdom using Weapons Effect Simulators (SAWES). These use eye-safe, low-powered lasers attached to weapons. These lasers represent the projectiles that would be fired for real, and detectors on both men and vehicles register 'kills' and near misses. The body-worn jacket is vectored into position; once hit, a siren sounds and the soldier must lie on his back to stop it. [UKLF]

86. A Milan team of a BAOR unit during the live-firing phase of an exercise. The man in the left background is holding a Milan tube, with end covers fitted, while the two in the foreground each hold an empty. Between them they carry the Milan by the support assembly; the white flash on the tripod leg indicates the forward leg; the handle above the tripod is the elevating handgrip; and to the tripod's right is the guidance electronic pack. On his back, the man at the right carries a rolled up sleeping-mat, evidence of an exercise lasting several days. [BAOR]

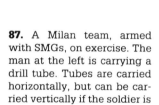

87. A Milan team, armed with SMGs, on exercise. The man at the left is carrying a drill tube. Tubes are carried horizontally, but can be carried vertically if the soldier is tall enough – it depends on battle balance. Milan rounds are pre-packaged; in combat the tube is discarded. The middle man is the No. 1 and carries the firing post on a GS carrier; for quicker response, the firing post can be carried directly on the back. The inner smock zipper can be seen. The nearer man has an SAS rucksack, made from OG nylon with an external frame with side pockets. [UKLF]

88. Members of the Royal Artillery operating a gun. The Helmet, Combat Mk 6 chin-strap gives a very firm grip. It replaced the 1944-pattern steel helmet. [UKLF]

89. Members of the Gordon Highlanders arriving in the Falklands with their full kit. They appear to have the SAS rucksack. By the 1970s, the Bergen's design and materials were obsolete so the 'Rucksack SAS' was designed to replace it. Made from OG nylon with an external frame, it has side pockets which could be stowed flat with press studs when empty, and provision to carry skis or entrenching tools behind the side pockets. Another more basic OG nylon, external-frame GS rucksack was issued later, in time to see service in the Falklands War, alongside a variety of privately purchased rucksacks. [UKLF]

90. Gordon Highlanders in the Falklands. Of interest are their 1958-pattern mugs, cap-comforters, scarves and cold weather DPM caps with flaps. [UKLF]

89

90

91. A GPMG position on the perimeter of Stanley Airfield manned by a KSLI soldier of BFFI during Exercise 'FTX' in November 1984. He is in CEFO, with a small pack. In CEFO, he might be carrying four SLR magazines in one ammo pouch, and three plus his weapon cleaning kit in the other (totalling seventy rounds) plus one belt (fifty rounds) of GPMG ammunition, two grenades, and bayonet and scabbard. In his kidney pouches (behind his ammo pouches), he might have his messtin, combat rations and knife/fork/spoon; washing/shaving kit and towel; footpowder, boot cleaning kit, spare socks and spare laces; and housewife. [KSLI, via G. Archer Parfitt]

92. A Royal Navy Sea King helicopter drops KSLI members of Exercise 'Green Skua' at Pegotty Bluff at the start of the march during the mid-1980s. They carry 'SAS Bergens'. The Falklands War influenced the design of the new load-carrying equipment which concentrates upon the rucksack and its comfortable carriage in line with the modern infantryman who modifies issue equipment for utility and comfort. Since the early 1980s, APRE Farnborough has been developing the equipment, with facilities to simulate conditions from jungle to arctic zones. It will take years to re-equip the infantry, let alone the entire British Army. [KSLI, via G. Archer Parfitt]

93. A member of UKLF on exercise in arid conditions on Cyprus during 1989, wearing No. 9 Dress DPMs (note the rolled-up sleeves and pockets), 1958-pattern equipment (note the pack clipped on at the right) and a khaki bush hat. He carries an LSW. [UKLF/ACE]

94

95

94. Lieutenant Owens and a member of her signals unit prepare to join the United Nations peace-keeping force in Namibia during 1989. Their job was to ensure vital communications. All ranks of all arms seconded to, on loan to, or on exchange with Commonwealth or foreign armies usually wear some or all of the dress of those forces, such as bush hats in Nigeria, Arab head-dress in the Gulf States, and always – as here – soldiers serving with UN peace-keeping forces adopt the UN blue beret. However, they retain 1958-pattern belt, wool pullover, tailored blouse, OG lightweight trousers, and black DMS boots laced straight across. [UKLF]

95. Typifying the combat clothing of the Modern British soldier, a Rigid Raider rider on patrol with the British Army of the Rhine (BAOR), wearing DPM No. 8 smock, woolly-pully and Combat Helmet Mk 6 with DPM cover with elastic

straps sewn on it for camo. He is armed with an SMG (not loaded) and is wearing a life-jacket. In the fore-ground are 25-litre fuel jerry cans; under the life-preserver is the winch. [BAOR]

96. Infantry from the ACE Mobile Force (Land) on winter exercise in Norway wearing white snow suits, white helmet covers over Mk 6 helmets and mittens. The use of helmet covers in-creases the utility of hel-mets. Three have SMGs, one an SA80, and they have ap-plied white tape strips to them to break up their out-line in the snow. [UKLF]

97. An artilleryman guards his 105mm during an exer-cise in Norway. He is wear-ing mittens, parka, snow over-trousers and over-shoes. He is armed with a Bren. The gun is beneath a winter camouflage net, and has been painted with black/white disruptive pat-tern. [UKLF]

98

99

98. These soldiers have SA80s with BFAs, and are wearing well-worked DPMs and Mk 6 helmets, and carry their NBC slung on their left hips. The soldier at the right front of this BAOR route march has inserted zips into his DMS boots: these zips have canvas-backing with lace holes down the edges which are laced into the boot lace holes. [BAOR]

99. With bulging breast pockets and camo-creamed face, a soldier of BAOR on exercise showing the rolled up bed-roll. Since the Falklands War, rucksack designers have abandoned the rigid, external-frame in favour of the flexible internal frame in most civilian designs. Such rucksacks include Berghaus designs supplied to the MoD by the company or purchased in great numbers by servicemen. In CEMO, a soldier might carry in his pack his beret, cap-comforter, drawers, spare KF shirts, socks, towel and gloves, his boot cleaning kit, and sleeping-bag and NBC suit. [BAOR]

100. A soldier of BAOR on exercise carrying his rolled up bed-roll on top of his radio. He wears a head-over and woollen gloves. Leather combat gloves have replaced knitted khaki gloves on general issue. Someone else will be carrying his pack. [BAOR]

101. An 84mm anti-tank team on exercise in a BAOR training area wearing plenty of vegetation in the elastic tapes on the DPM-covers of their Mk 6 helmets. For getting in close, such camo is essential. [BAOR]

102. Two signallers, line-layers, lay a DIO line. They wear NBC Black. NBC kit makes any task more difficult, but it is troops poorly trained in NBC who need to wear more protection as it takes them longer to reach State Black. The new dress categories are: NBC Zero – full IPE carried; One – wearing suit, carrying respirator, boots and gloves; Two – wearing overboots and suit with hood down, carrying respirator and gloves; Three – wearing overboots, gloves and suit with hood up; Black – wearing full IPE. To any of one, two or three can be suffixed 'R' for respirator, and 'F' for facelet mask (for drivers and sleepers). [BAOR]

103. 'A sucking wound is nature's way of saying you lost the firefight . . .', but this is an RAMC simulation during a BAOR exercise and he's a much too happy teddy. The first field dressing used to be kept in a specially-designed pocket on the right side of the groin which — clear evidence, some soldiers said, that the suit was designed by a woman — meant that one had a large lump pressing against the testicles when you lay down! So it was then carried in the top left-hand pocket; and on the new jackets there is a pocket for it on the right arm. [BAOR]

104. This is an RAMC simulation of treating a casualty during an NBC phase of a I Corps exercise. The attendants are wearing full IPE (Individual Protective Equipment) which gives nearly 100 per cent protection, and the one at the right has detector paper on his/her left forearm. Battle casualties are inevitable, but since the issue of full IPE British commanders will accept no chemical casualties. The dread effects of chemical agents are 'SLUD': Salivate, Lachyrmate, Urinate, Defecate. [BAOR]

105. A tank driver of a BAOR regiment, wearing his AFV crewman's helmet with built-in earphone/microphone communication set, plus his goggles with nose and mouthpiece protective pieces, and under it all a heavy woollen balaclava. The 'Dan Dare' helmet is manufactured by Racal Communications. [BAOR]

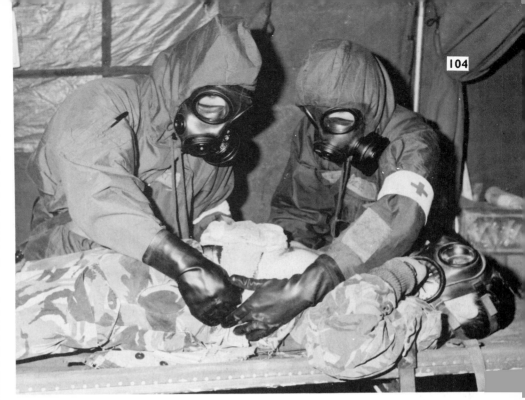

104

105

106. An APC commander of a BAOR unit during a winter in Germany, wearing light-weight hard hat with radio and face protection, and a parka, and no doubt his warmest 'shreddies' (underwear). [BAOR]

107. The men changing the engine of an MBT of the RTR in BAOR are wearing DPM boots, but are not wearing full No. 12 Protective Overalls. They are wearing their black berets. [Tank Museum]

108. Royal Armoured Corps MBT crew wearing their dark blue berets and AFV crewman's denim overalls. [BAOR]

109. Refuelling action from a well-netted tanker in BAOR by men in full No. 8 DPM suits but without headgear although they are wearing ear protectors against engine and pump noise. [BAOR]

110. This soldier on traffic control duty is wearing a high-visibility smock over a DPM smock and under 1958-pattern webbing. He is carrying an SMG slung. [BAOR]

111. Wearing an identity card and a worsted embroidered rank patch on his shoulder, this RTR staff-sergeant wears black beret, scrim scarf and 'old'-pattern DPM blouse. He is at a base in Germany and appears to be taking an inventory of extruded aluminium planking, developed for use during maintenance and other tasks in Germany where the soil load bearing is light. [BAOR]

112. A member of the WRAC serving with BAOR, under-taking Umpire duty – white armband – during an exercise in Germany. The chain for her whistle, in the field-dressing pocket, is clipped to the jacket button. [BAOR]

113. British Army Berlin meets US Army Berlin (Rangers). The uniform worn by the Berlin Brigade is the same as worn by the rest of the British Army serving in the United Kingdom and BAOR. There are no items, features or embellishments which are specific to Berlin, but the insignia of the Berlin Brigade (the so-called 'Flaming Arsehole') is among the few items allowed by Regulations to be worn on the smock. [Army PI, Berlin Section, photo. Mike Kline]

114. Personnel of the British Army Berlin, from 14/20th Hussars (right); Light Infantry (centre); and a Scottish regiment, conferring. Frankle wears his 1958 equipment loose. Frankle and the Scot wear the 'old pattern' DPM jacket, far superior to the new-issue jacket. A medium-weight jacket, it is well made from tough fabric with a full poplin lining and four flat, good size, sewn outer pockets on the front, a pen pocket on the left sleeve, and an internal map pocket – even a poacher's large pocket sewn inside the lower back. It has good weather resistance, with tightly buttoned cuffs and a heavy-duty zip in a storm flap, and the lining gives added wind-resistance. However, if the jacket gets soaked it becomes very heavy and the poplin lining will stay wet long after the outside has dried. [Army PI, Berlin Section, photo. Henrik G. Pastor]

115. His HEAT slung, an anti-tank soldier of British Army Berlin is abseiling. Below him are others. The 'new issue' trousers have box-sewn pockets – when an infantryman is crawling or climbing, these can snag and rip off; and when a machine-gunner is carrying his LMG, his linked rounds catch on the edge and break off. That can be a curse in a firing competition, for the gunner will end up with just five rounds to fire instead of a belt which will be lying on the ground 300 metres away! One infantry fire-team became known as the 'band-aid' team because their officer taped their LMG number's leg pockets to prevent them snagging his link! [Army PI, Berlin Section, British Army Berlin]

116. CSM, Cfm, and a private of the Argyll and Sutherland Highlanders, on duty in Ulster, wearing various No. 8 Dress garments. [A&SH]

117. Showing the front and the back of the 'flak jacket' worn in Northern Ireland, 1st Battalion, The Argyll and Sutherland Highlanders, mid-1980s in Northern Ireland. Throughout the campaign, troops have been issued with the 'vest, frag-mentation' of ballistic nylon fabric which weighs just one pound per square foot – light enough to let soldiers move freely. It has saved many from injury by 'bricks and stones' and even low-velocity, but not high-velocity, bullets. Only cer-amic armour can do that, but this weighs six times as much, making it too clumsy for infantry, except those on static OP or sentry duty, and it only protects the heart, lungs and spine. However, a Kevlar armoured vest has also been designed; Kevlar, first used by NASA, is light yet has splendid anti-ballis-tic properties. The flak jacket remains the only compromise until the SCRDE produces a lightweight fully protective body armour. The vests here are of the early pattern; later ones have non-slip shoulder-pads and lower pockets. [A&SH]

118. A member of the 4th Battalion, KSLI on foot patrol in Northern Ireland, during the 1970s. In positions like this, the point to the padded backs of the North Ireland gloves is evident. [KSLI TA, via G. Archer Parfitt]

119. A support company of the 1st Battalion, The Argyll and Sutherland Highlanders on patrol in Northern Ireland during the early 1980s. Northern Ireland confronts infantry with several problems of fire, movement and protection – flak vest are not the only solution and cover and mutual protection must be used efficiently. [A&SH]

120. A Royal Army Veterinary Corps Specialist dog-handler working in Northern Ireland, c. 1985. The soldier wears Combats and Cromwell Helmet with visor and Mk 1 Boots Combat High. He is armed with the 9mm Browning pistol. A German Shepherd AES (Arms Explosive Search) dog is being 'cast' in the direction of the intended clearance. The dog harness signifies to the animal that it is working. The glass-reinforced Combat Helmet Northern Ireland was developed very quickly. It is lighter than the steel helmet and has better ballistic and shock protection and easier fit. The wide chin-strap protects the chin. The visor is acid-proof. [Royal Army Veterinary Corps]

121. Gurkha engineers prepare a defensive position during an exercise in the United Kingdom, but the terrorist threats to military installations in the UK and BAOR meant that many bases were fortified. A Gurkha hat is two sewn together. They are wearing new-issue DPM jackets with lightweight trousers, in the special sizes made for the compact Gurkha figure. [UKLF]

122. I Corps troops in full NBC kit being decontaminated during training. The Chemical Safety Rule is drummed into soldiers: 'If you Experience a bombardment of any kind; Sight hostile or unknown low-flying aircraft; See suspicious mist, smoke droplets or splashes; Smell anything unusual; Notice symptoms of the effects of agents in yourself or others, such as dimness of vision, irritation of the eyes, sudden headaches, tightness of the chest, running nose and intense salivation, or Hear the NBC alarm – then you must assume that it is a chemical attack and carry out the immediate action drill.' [UKLF]

123. An Officer Cadet of the WRAC models the full Women's No. 8 Dress Temperate Combat Suit, with DPM shoulder-bag cover Mk I fitted, and wearing 1958-pattern web belt, combat boots high with khaki woollen puttees and a khaki poplin shirt. [WRAC]

124. The soldier on the left is wearing full combat kit; the soldier on the right is wearing the most recent pattern of NBC kit. They have the latest model of equipment. Testing of new designs over several years led to large-scale user trials in the late 1980s, but it will take years to re-equip the infantry, let alone the entire Army. High-quality materials and finish are used. For swift NBC decontamination, the equipment is made from polyurethane-coated textured nylon with hard nylon buckles and fastenings (like commercial equipment). Although using the 1958 belt and yoke concept, the back is uncluttered to allow a rucksack to be carried in comfort, with a nylon mesh panel as the back of the yoke. The new rucksack, the first on general issue, has an internal frame, shoulder- and waist-straps and an expandable capacity. The large side pockets can be unzipped from the main envelope, and either zipped together or used singly (the man at the right), and the rucksack can be used with single, double or no side pockets, allowing loads ranging from basic essentials to those for extended hard-country patrolling to be carried. [UKLF]

125

126

125. Contrast the styles of dress of these Royal Scots Dragoon Guards at Lumsden Barracks in Germany: the crew's new-style tankers' coverall and two styles of boot; the inspecting officer's DMS boots, DPM smock and lightweight slacks; the attending officers are wearing boots and shoes and overalls. The crew are wearing blue berets, although RSDG are entitled to grey as are the attending officers at left. The many sizes that must be kept of several dress orders means that the quartermaster's stores of a relatively small regiment must resort to tailoring because, although the mean height and weight of the British soldier is 5ft 8½in and 10 stones 7 oz, not only are there many variations either side, but soldiers grow out of their clothes – many enlist at seventeen. It is the task of the Director of Clothing and Textiles (DCT), with HQ in the Old War Office Building, to ensure the basic clothing supply. [Royal Scots Dragoon Guards]

126. Two Royal Scots Dragoon Guards on the range, with SA80s, wearing DPM jackets, lightweight trousers, and DPM boots and ear protectors – a wise precaution; many older soldiers are hard of hearing and a deaf soldier is a dead soldier. They wear their equipment in two different styles. In CEFO, a soldier normally carries two ammo pouches, two kidney pouches, rolled poncho, waterbottle, pick/ shovel, sandbag, respirator and NBC gear. In recent years, the fashion of SAS 'belt order' has spread. [Royal Scots Dragoon Guards]

127. Close co-operation between Chieftain tanks and Saxon armoured personnel carriers – battle taxis – is essential during infantry assaults. These infantry are equipped with SAWES. These Light Infantry wear full No. 8 DPM Dress, with 1958-pattern webbing. The main design fault of the 1958 pattern is that a rucksack and radio cannot be carried on the back with comfort in CEMO, but it can be carried in CEFO – the design favours the APC-borne infantryman. The first soldier out has a smaller, folding en- trenching tool strapped across his bum-roll – this has been replacing the original 1958 rigid tool, and many soldiers have cut off the web attachments for the tool to make for easier carriage of a pack. [UKLF]

128. During 'Desert Shield', a woman corporal of 7th Armoured Division, seen wearing tropical No. 9 DPM in short-sleeve order, over a combat vest, with 1958 webbing and pouches and issue watch. She is armed with an SMG. Her rank is on her right sleeve, embroidered on a brown patch, below the division's Desert Rat insignia. [British Army]

129

130

129. Three medical officers, all captains, attached to 7th Armoured Division, pose outside their field hospital while taking part in 'Desert Shield'. They are wearing DPMs in short-sleeve order and boonie hats, with their medic armbands on the left arm; only two are wearing No. 9 DPM Tropical suits. The officer in the centre is wearing the Desert Rat insignia on her right arm. Her 1958-pattern webbing belt is visible, but the others are not wearing webbing belts. The officer at the left has a large nylon medical bag slung at her hip with a nylon web around her waist. They are wearing their rank – khaki embroidered pips – on DPM-slides on their epaulettes. [British Army]

130. During 'Desert Shield', two medical orderlies of QARANC check the supply state. They are wearing lightweight DPMs. [British Army]

131. Two British Army doctors in Saudi Arabia with the 'Desert Shield' forces, the male wearing the Desert DPMs, and the female tropical DPMs. [British Army]

132. A QARANC nurse attends to a squaddie in a field hospital. Both are wearing Tropical DPM. The young soldier shows off his shreddie (vest), a modern web belt and buckle and a wrist sweatband; his boonie hat has fallen off. The nurse is wearing her rank – corporal – on a shoulder-slide. [British Army]

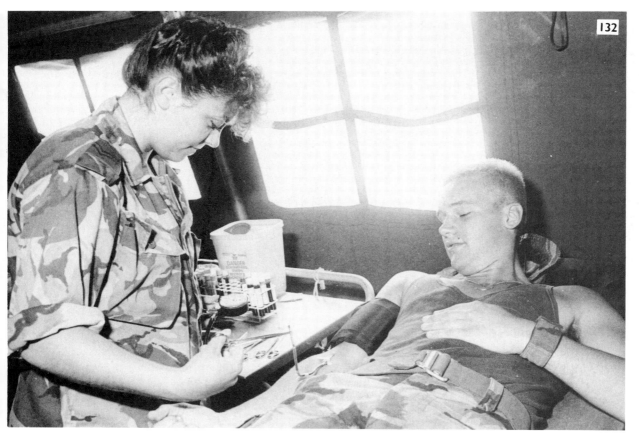

133

134

133. 'Desert Shield' keep-fit class. Four British soldiers fill sandbags. Seen before the proper gear had arrived, they wear sweatshirts, lightweight DPMs and DMS boots. British soldiers wearing DMS boots suffered sores and blisters and wrote home asking their families to buy desert boots and send them because the existing boots let in the sand. [British Army]

134. Saudi Arabia, 1991, but it could almost be Libya, 1941. A soldier of 7th Armoured Division brews-up with bottled water beside his Challenger MBT. He wears Desert DPMs, and DMS boots. [British Army]

135. 'Desert Storm'. An infantry commander leads his men forward down a natural trench. They wear Desert DPMs in stone, with matching covers for their Helmets Combat Mk 6. The officer is carrying his PRC on his back on a brace. His rifle has been painted sand, now weathered through use. He has his short bayonet fixed. He is wearing the new Boots, Desert, Combat which were designed, tested and into production within weeks of the need for a special boot being realized. The boot weighs 1lb 2oz – a full 1lb lighter than the DMS. It has a suede foot, a canvas tongue which is double stitched to stop sand getting in, and a high canvas ankle. It has a thermoplastic heel counter for greater strength and a synthetic moulded toepiece. It has a synthetic leather board insole and nitrile rubber sole. The eyelets are of enamelled brass. [British Army]

136. 'Desert Storm'. Two Desert Rat infantrymen assess their next move. They are wearing the 'stone' Desert DPMs and helmet cover, and the new desert boots. They carry SA80s with night sights. Both are wearing non-issue webbing. The nearer is the radio operator, and holds his telephone in his left hand. [British Army]

GROUPS OF DRESS

The British Army defines temperate zones as the United Kingdom and north-west Europe, and Warm-Weather zones as Brunei, Canada, Caribbean, Hong Kong, Mediterranean, Nepal and the United States. The orders of dress authorized for servicemen of the British Army are as follows:

Full Dress is the traditional dress of the Household troops when carrying out public duties. Full dress and ceremonial items for wear with it are provided at public expense by the RAOC for The Household Cavalry; The King's Troop, RHA; and The Guards Division. Although declared obsolete for the rest of the Army, it can be obtained at regimental expense for wear on certain occasions, such as by bands, corps of drums, pipers and trumpeters.

No. 1 Dress, Blues: Temperate Ceremonial Uniform. No. 1 Dress is seen less frequently than No. 2 Dress and full dress for bands which are mostly used on ceremonial parades. Unlike the older dress, the new 1947 pattern Blues were never popular with the Army from their introduction in the early 1950s; it resembles the uniform of railway porters and postmen. No. 1 Dress is issued at public expense to soldiers, but must be purchased by officers from their uniform allowance. It may be supplied for wear on 'appropriate occasions'. It is issued on permanent basis to certain troops – including all senior ranks, bandsmen, drummers, buglers and pipers; the RMP; the Royal Signals motorcycle display team; and Sandhurst cadets. With heavy, repeated price rises for cotton, wool and leather over the past two decades, the Army has had constantly to review its clothing budgets, and not unreasonably No. 1 Dress is now worn only by soldiers who have special ceremonial duties.

No. 2 Dress Temperate Service Dress. Standard drab ('khaki') temperate parade uniform worn since 1960, No. 2 Dress was originally parade and working uniform for many soldiers, i.e., office staff, instructors, etc. It consists of coloured forage cap, skirted khaki jacket, shirt, collar and tie, khaki trousers, brown shoes (officers) or black boots (ORs); Scottish regiments wear Glengarry, jacket with cutaway skirts, trews or kilt and diced hose. Shirtsleeve order was not officially approved, but No. 2 Dress was worn with sleeves rolled down, and tie retained. Sometimes 'pullover order' was worn with No. 2 Dress trousers and by officers with SD trousers. No. 2 Dress is issued on a scale of one suit for every soldier, except for some personnel – including Guards, MPs and Recruiters – who require two for special duties.

No. 3 Dress Warm-Weather Ceremonial Uniform. The white cotton version of No. 1 Dress, No. 3 Dress is supplied for warm-weather areas principally for bands, corps of drums and buglers. The scale of issue is two suits.

No. 4 Dress Officers Warm-Weather Service Dress. No. 4 Dress is made in stone-coloured polyester and wool worsted and styled like its temperate equivalent, No. 2 Dress. It is for wear in warm-weather areas on formal occasions, except on parade with troops. It is worn over a shirt and tie.

No. 5 Dress Battledress. This was last listed in 1969 Regulations, and is now obsolete.

No. 6 Dress Warm-Weather Parade Uniform. No. 6 Dress is worn for ceremonial and formal parade purposes in warm-weather areas by officers and ORs. It equates to No. 2 Dress, whose head-dress and accoutrements apply. The open-necked bush jacket in stone polyester and cotton may be worn with or without a shirt and tie. Scottish regiments wear Highland-pattern jacket with trews or kilt and hose.

No. 7 Dress Warm-Weather Barrack Dress. No. 7 Dress is a work uniform in warm-weather areas and consists of stone short-sleeve shirt and trousers worn with web belt, service dress cap, beret or TOS.

No. 8 Dress Temperate Disruptive Pattern Material (DPM) Combat Dress. This Order and No. 2 Dress form the modern British soldier's basic kit, and is the same for all ranks. The successor to the combat clothing issued during the Korean War, the original Combat Dress was first issued in 1970 in plain OG, and the second pattern in DPM was introduced in 1972 since when there have been several patterns of DPM temperate combat dress. It consists of beret, bonnet TOS or DPM helmet, DPM combat smock or blouse and DPM or OG trousers, and DMS boots, combat, high. There is a DPM waterproof smock and trousers and special combat smocks for parachutists and the SAS. Shirtsleeve-order is also worn with combat dress trousers. Two suits per man are issued for field wear in temperate areas. Regulations demand KF shirts, but officer pattern and No. 2 Dress shirts are also worn unofficially. WOs rank badges are worn on green cotton wristband; some have metal badges, others cloth. In poor weather DPM jackets are worn officially or otherwise with barrack dress; this became very common after issues of the Army raincoat ceased.

No. 9 Dress Tropical Disruptive Pattern Material (DPM) Combat Dress. Introduced in 1976, No. 9 Dress is the tropical version of No. 8 Dress in a lightweight DPM. It consists of DPM soft bush hat, DPM tropical jacket and trousers, and boots DMS with short puttees or jungle boots. Three suits per man are issued for field wear in warm-weather areas.

No. 10 Dress Temperate Mess Dress. No. 10 Dress is worn by Officers, WOs and senior NCOs (optional for WOs and NCOs) in their messes on formal occasions. The style of 'mess dress' reflects regimental tradition, with those regiments entitled to the red coat wearing it and Scottish regiments wearing kilt and trews.

No. 11 Dress Warm-Weather Mess Dress. The warm-weather version of No. 10 Dress, No. 11 Dress is worn by Officers, WOs and sergeants only (but is optional for WOs and NCOs) and usually includes a lightweight white drill jacket and waistcoat, or regimental cummerbund.

No. 12 Dress Protective Clothing. No. 12 Dress covers orders of dress falling under the general description of 'protective clothing' from 'Coveralls, Flame-resistant, AFV Crewman' and 'Coveralls, Man's Black, RTR' of the RAC, through special items for RA, RE, REME, Royal Signals, RCT and RAOC to cooks', butchers', dentists' and surgeons' clothing.

No. 13 Dress Temperate Barrack Dress. No. 13 Dress is worn in barracks in temperate areas when No. 2 Dress is not required, and it is interchangeable with No. 14 Dress. Since the 1960s, basic barrack dress has been green trousers and khaki sweater, but it may include jersey; light-weight, dark khaki-green; terylene trousers; combat trousers; kilt or trews; barrack dress trousers or No. 2 trousers, and KF, No. 2 or officer pattern shirt with heavy woollen pullover. Although combinations of hats, caps, kilts, trousers, etc., are legion, the one common item is the 'jersey, wool, heavy', the famous 'woolly-pully'. All regiments wear canvas belts in regimental designs, but most regiments have kept other variations. Sweaters have been blue, green, maroon and grey: Royal Signals have dark blue sweaters, Royal Hampshires black, Cheshire Regiment brown and Intelligence Corps green.

No. 14 Dress Shirt-Sleeve Order. Interchangeable with No. 13 Dress, No. 14 Dress is No. 13 Dress without the woolly-pully, 'shirt sleeve' order, worn in summer in temperate areas. This order is also worn with light-weight green cotton trousers. Shirt-Sleeve Order with Battledress Trousers usually consists of KF shirt with sleeves rolled up and no tie, although some officers and WOIs keep the tie on. WOs'

badges have been worn on a wristband, usually leather with metal badge. WOIs may wear the officer-pattern shirt. Sometimes, the old-type V-necked pullover has been worn over the shirt.

Basic Issue. Although the number of extras and variations is legion, the basic kit issued to a modern British soldier is based on Nos. 2 and 8 Dress and includes: one No. 2 Dress (khaki jacket and trousers); two No. 8 Dress Combat Suits (DPM jacket and trousers); two pairs of green barrack-room trousers; two pullovers; two khaki poplin shirts; one beret; one No. 1 Dress Cap (usually dark blue); three thick khaki shirts (combat wear); two pairs of DMS boots, combat, high; one pair of shoes; and four pairs of socks.

MODEL FIGURES

There have been model soldiers for as long as there have been soldiers, but the quality of detail, the range and the availability of today's model soldier has never been rivalled. The excellent Britain's full-scale soldiers were swamped by the cheap Airfix OO/HO polystyrene figures in the 1960s; other plastic kit manufacturers followed such as Heller and ESCI. These were mainly for small boys and wargamers. Larger-scale figures followed. Both ends of the plastics spectrum remain popular, but the following list does not go into the polystyrene figure market because, though it is vast, there are few figures relevant to the post-war British Army to be found in a model shop or in manufacturers' catalogues.

The arrival in the late 1970s of firms selling reasonably priced, finely detailed, large-scale figures in white-metal alloy again changed the nature and direction of figure modelling. Now, in the 1990s, there are several dozen companies – hardly 'cottage industries' any longer – producing between them several thousand figures covering the length and breadth of military history in a number of scales.

It is upon these companies that the following survey of model figures in British combat garb since 1945 concentrates. Whereas there are many in the later forms of combat dress, there are few figures in battledress of the post-war period, so the list includes figures in Second World War dress that fit the bill, with a bit of conversion.

Prices vary from three or four pounds sterling to fifteen pounds, depending upon scale and complexity. The price given is a guide only – stabilized on the first day of the first month of the first year of the new decade, the nineties! Check with the manufacturers' latest catalogues before purchasing.

Most of the specialist model companies sell by mail order (cheque, Postal Order, Access or Visa), and there are several mail order shops from whom goods that prove hard to get locally can be bought. Modeltoys of Portsmouth offer a wide range by mail order. E. D. Models of Solihull import ranges and sell on the premises and by mail; notable among their wares are Chota Sahib and Cheshire Volunteers. Historex Agents sell Ara Miniatures, Andrea Miniatures, Verlinden, Barton Miniatures, Cheshire Volunteers, Mil-Art and Tiny Troopers. Tradition sell their own Tradition series and Squadron. Vandrad handle the MLR and Hotspur 20mm wargaming figures.

The monthly magazine *Military Modelling* (MAP) is indispensable for the military figure modeller. The modelling

press records new releases of figures and accessories in articles, reviews and advertisements. It also gives figure manufacturers' addresses and prices of catalogues. For full details of the range of a manufacturer, buy their catalogue from a model shop or through the mail for a couple of pounds; smaller firms' product lists are often available (send a self-addressed stamped envelope).

Modelling is no longer limited to polystyrene plastics. A few of the 'mainstream' model companies – such as ESCI – manufacture figures in the larger scales in polystyrene, but most specialist manufacturers use white-metal alloy to achieve the very fine casting demanded by modellers today; some accessories are in resin and etched brass. Figures are in kit form, but usually with the minimum of parts, and some are in one piece. They usually come with a metal base, but some come with a wooden base to be stained or varnished.

The best way to assemble white-metal items is with Isocyanoacylate glue – 'Superglue' – which will bond both similar and dissimilar products rapidly and strongly. It is also far less of an immediate health risk than polysolvent. (Nevertheless, all powerful glues should be treated as health hazards, as the manufacturers warn: contact with skin, inhalation and exposing eyes to vapour should be avoided in case of long-term effects.) 'Second Generation' Superglue comes in bottles that do not tip, with a nozzle that does not clog – gone is the use-once-and-discard tube whose contents stuck its cap on! It can be thin for coverage, or thick to fill gaps between components.

For constructing white-metal kits and accessories, it is useful to learn to solder with low-melt solder which gives a very strong bond and also fills the gaps between components as you go rather than having to go back over it with filler after assembling with glue. The correct kind of soldering iron, adjustable to specific low temperatures, must be used, and good-quality low-melt solder and flux, such as Carrs Red Label. A good railway model shop should provide both products and advice on techniques.

After gluing, fill any gaps with Milliput Fine or WP Epoxy Putty. Casting in white-metal may leave 'flash' or mould lines to be removed. This is done with a very sharp craft knife and fine file, and 'wet 'n' dry' graphite paper. Fine wire wool, toothpaste, Brasso or very fine grinding compound can be used to prepare or restore finishes for painting and help to eliminate 'bubbling'; some modellers use a small suede brush. Some parts – like weapon slings – will have to be bent to shape, which must be done very carefully to avoid distortion or breakage.

After assembling and cleaning up the figure, it should be undercoated. Car spray grey primer gives a very smooth finish and also fills any minute holes; thinned grey enamel works equally well. Although preparation is vitally impor-

tant, it is in the painting that the model is really 'made'. Thinned enamels, water-based paints, acrylic paints, inks and oil paints can all be used to give various effects. Manufacturers and instructions can be found in the modelling press and in several specific publications.

ADDRESSES

Ara Miniatures, Fundisimo, S. L. Maximo Aguirre 10, 2 48011 Bilbao, Spain

Chota Sahib, 25 St Paul's Street, Brighton, Sussex BN2 3HR

Clydecast Products, 97 Fereneze Avenue, Clarkston, Glasgow G76 7RT; Tel. (041) 638-1904

E. D. Models, 64 Stratford Road, Shirley, Solihull, West Midlands B90 3LP; Tel. (021) 744-7488

Gerry Ford Design, 43 Queens Road, Farnborough, Hants GU14 6JP

Hearne Miniatures, 10 Friars Walk, Exeter EX2 4AY

Helmet Soldiers, 12 Harrington Close, Windsor SL4 4AD

Historex Agents, 3 Castle Street, Dover, Kent CT16 1QJ; Tel. (0304) 206720

Hornet Models, P.O. Box 64, Rochester, Kent ME1 3JR

Hyde Diecasting, Unit One, Providence Mill, Alexandra Street, Hyde, Cheshire SK14 1DX

Langley Models, 166 Three Bridges Road, Crawley, Sussex RH10 1LE

Mac's Models, 168 Canongate, Royal Mile, Edinburgh EH8 8DF; Tel. (031) 557 5551

Miniatures Andrea, Josea Diaz 12, 28038 Madrid, Spain

New Hope Design, Tynwald Mill, St John's, Isle of Man; Tel. (0624) 71392/71529

Phoenix Model Developments Ltd, The Square, Earls Barton, Northampton NN6 ONA; Tel. (Northampton) 810612

Series 77, c/o Tangley Model Workshop, 89b/89c Woodbridge Road, Guildford, Surrey

Spencer Smith Miniatures, 5, Barrowgate Road, London W4 4QX

Tradition, 5a, Shepherd Street, Mayfair, London W1

Vandrad, 7 Marpool Hill, Exmouth, East Devon EX8 2LJ; Tel. (0395) 278664

DISPLAY CASES

Anchor Green Ltd, Regency House, Shrewsbury SY5 9JW; Tel. (074) 383 246

Craft Supplies, Dept MM, Millers Dale, Buxton, Derbyshire SK17 BSN; Tel. (0298) 871636

Formation Plastix, Unit E4, Hilton Main Small Business Park, Featherstone, Staffordshire; Tel. (0902) 723999

PAINTS

Rose Model Paints (via New Hope)
[water-based]: White, Black, Flesh, Light/Dark Green, Light/Dark Blue, Brown, Yellow Ochre, Scarlet, Crimson, Yellow, Antique/Rich Gold Powder, Silver; Powder-Mixing Medium £1.00

FIGURES

The prices shown are an indication only; purchasers showed check the authorized selling price with the retailer or manufacturer.

Code	Description	Price
BARTON MINIATURES		
90mm		
BM/H2	Private, Parachute Regt, Patrol Order 1984	£14.25
BM/H3	Royal Marine, Patrol Order, 1984	14.25
BM/H4	Trooper, SAS, Operation 'Nimrod', 1980	14.25
BM/H5	Private, Parachute Regt, Falklands, 1982	15.85
BM/H8	Private, Black Watch, IS role, 1983	14.85
BM/H9	Private, RAMC, Falklands, 1982	14.25
BM/H11	Trooper, SAS, Falklands, 1982	15.85
BM/H12	Private, Queen's Own Highlanders, Falklands, 1983	15.85
BM/H13	Private, The Parachute Regt, Drop Order, 1984	15.85
H/19	Bombardier, Royal Artillery, with Javelin	14.25
H14	Private, Parachute Regt, Arctic, skis	15.85
H20	Soldier, IS Role, Riot Dress, helmet, baton	15.85

1/35th Scale		
BM/301	Royal Armoured Corps Tank Commander, 1990	£2.95
BM/302	Royal Armoured Corps Tank Crewman, 1990	2.95
BM/303	Royal Armoured Corps Tank Crewman, 1990	2.95
BM/304	Royal Armoured Corps Officer, 1990	2.95
CHESHIRE VOLUNTEERS		
54mm		
MN4	Private, 1st Queen's Dragoon Guards	£4.25
BA1	Private, Infantry, Combat Order, 1988	4.25
BA4	Private, Combat Order, Falklands, 1982	4.25
CHOTA SAHIB		
54mm		
BI/6	Royal Regt of Fusiliers, 1977	£4.25
BI/7	Corporal, WRAC Military Police, 1975	4.25
BI/8	2nd Lieutenant, QARANC, 1978	4.25
BI/9	Argyll & Sutherland Highlander, 1970s	4.25

BI/10	Ammunition Technician Officer, N. Ireland, 1977	4.25
BI/17	SAS, Operation 'Nimrod'	4.25
BI/20	3 Infantrymen, N. Ireland, 1980s	12.75
BI/21	Sergeant, Royal Marines, 1980	4.25
BI/22	Corporal RMP, N. Ireland, 1969–84	4.25
BI/24	Private, Parachute Regt/Lieutenant, RAMC, NW Europe, 1944	4.25
BI/25	Paratrooper, N. Ireland, 1977	4.25
TF/1	1/7th Gurkhas, Falklands, 1982	4.25
TF/2	Parachute Regt, Falklands, 1982	4.25
TF/3	Royal Marine, Falklands, 1982	4.25
TF/6	SBS, Falklands, 1982	4.25

CLYDECAST
75mm
SG21	Private, Scots Guards, 1979	£5.95
CCF26	Royal Marine, Winter Combat Dress, 1982	5.95
CCF39	British Infantryman, NW Europe, 1944	5.95
CCF58	British Infantryman, IS Duties, N. Ireland, 1980s	5.95

HEARNE MINIATURES
55mm
HM65-1	HALO Jumper, 22nd SAS Regt	£8.50

HORNET MODELS
1/35th
BH1	Military Policeman, directing traffic, 1939–45	£4.25
BH2	Infantryman, 1937 Battledress, Sidecap	4.25
BH3	Infantryman, kit, No. 4 rifle levelled, Mk III helmet	4.25
BH4	Infantryman, kit, No. 4 rifle at trail, Mk II helmet	4.25
BH5	Paratrooper, No. 4 rifle, jump helmet	4.25

HOTSPUR
20mm
Operation 'Corporate', 1982
CORP 1	Royal Marine, SBS	£1.35
CORP 2	Royal Marine, Arctic & Mountain Warfare Cadre	1.35
CORP 3	Infantryman	1.35
CORP 4	Infantryman	1.35
CORP 5	Infantry Commander	0.85

Police & Terrorist
URBN 2	SAS CRW	1.35
URBN 7	Private, IS Duties	1.35

MIL-ART
30mm
711	Trooper, 22nd SAS Regt, Falklands, 1982	£8.50
728	Trooper, 22nd SAS Regt, Oman, 1973	8.50
742	Infantryman, Combat Dress, 1987	9.75

MLR
20mm
British and Dominion Infantry, Mediterranean Theatre 1940–5
DOM 1	Command Group	£0.85
DOM 2	Advancing Infantryman	0.85
DOM 3	Firing Infantryman	0.85
DOM 4	Advancing Infantryman	0.85
DOM 5	Bren Group	0.85
DOM 6	Anti-Tank Group	0.85
DOM 7	2-inch Mortar Team	0.85
DOM 8	Bren Group	0.85
DOM 9	Pioneers	0.85
DOM 10	Support Group	0.85
DOM 11	Covering Infantryman	0.85
DOM 12	Carrier Crew on Foot	0.85
DOM 13	Infantry Casualties	0.85

NEW HOPE
1/32nd Scale [except *65mm; †90mm]
'Men-At-Arms' Series
MA031	Rifleman, 2nd Gurkha Rifles, Tropical Combat Dress, 1968	£4.25
MA032	Infantryman, Summer Dress Riot Gear (flak jacket), 1977	4.25
MA155*	Corporal, 1st Royal Hampshire Regt, Malaya, 1954	5.66
MA156*	WO, Royal Irish Rangers, Combat Dress, BAOR, 1974	5.66
MA190	Lance-Corporal, Gloucestershire Regt, Denims, 1961	4.25
MA201	Trooper, Rhodesian SAS, 1979	4.25
MA204	Trooper, 22nd SAS Regt, Oman, 1970	4.25
MA207	Trooper, 23rd SAS Regt, Combat Dress, 1982	4.25
MA323	Infantry Signaller, Malaya, 1951	4.25
MA324	Sikh Police Sergeant, Jungle Squad, Malaya, 1951	4.25
MA497†	NCO, 2nd Bn, Parachute Regt, Belize, 1983	12.77
MA498†	Private, 3rd Bn, Parachute Regt, Combat Order, 1981	12.77
MA517	Rigid Raider Coxswain, Falklands, 1982	4.25
MA520†	Trooper, 22nd SAS Regt, BCME, Operation 'Nimrod'	12.77

PHOENIX
75mm – 1/24th Scale
K5	Lance-Corporal, Military Police, NW Europe, 1944	£7.98
K7	Grenadier Guardsman, Drill Order, Battledress, 1944	7.98
K8	Grenadier Guardsman, Drill Order, Battledress, 1944	7.98
K9	English Infantryman, NW Europe, 1944	7.98
K10	Scottish Infantryman, NW Europe, 1944	7.98

TINY TROOPERS
90mm
TT/RTR1	Trooper, 3rd Royal Tank Regt, 1986	£12.75

VERLINDEN
1/35th
363	British Artillery Officer, 1939–5	£4.75

GLOSSARY AND ABBREVIATIONS

AAC	Army Air Corps	DPM	Disruptive Pattern Material	QM	Quartermaster
ACE	Allied Command Europe	FIBUA	Fighting In Built-Up Areas	RA	Royal Artillery
AES	Arm Explosive Research	GDS	Garment Development Section,	RAC	Royal Armoured Corps
AFV	Armoured Fighting Vehicle		Woolwich	RAMC	Royal Army Medical Corps
APC	Armoured Personnel Carrier	GPMG	General-Purpose Machine-Gun	RAOC	Royal Army Ordnance Corps
APRE	Army Personnel Research	GS	General Service	RAVC	Royal Army Veterinary Corps
	Establishment, Farnborough	HBT	Herring-Bone Twill (US)	RCT	Royal Corps of Transport
APTC	Army Physical Training Corps	HE	High-Explosive	REME	Royal Electrical and Mechanical
A&SH	Argyll and Sutherland	HEAT	High-Explosive Anti-Tank		Engineers
	Highlanders	IS	Internal Security	RHA	Royal Horse Artillery
ATO	Ammunition Technical Officer	ISBR	Individual Battle Skill Range	RM	Royal Marines
BAOR	British Army of the Rhine	IW	Individual Weapon	RMP	Royal Military Police
BATUS	British Army Training Unit	JG	Jungle-Green	RTR	Royal Tank Regiment
	Suffield	KD	Khaki Drill	RUR	Royal Ulster Rifles
BFA	Blank-Firing Attachment	KF	Khaki Flannel	SAS	Special Air Service
BFFD	British Forces Falklands Islands	KOSB	King's Own Scottish Borderers	SAWES	SA Weapons Effect Simulator
BHE	Battle Hardening Exercise	KSLI	King's [Shropshire] Light	SCRDE	Stores and Clothing Research
Bn	Battalion		Infantry		and Development
Cap FS	Cap, Field Service	LSW	Light Support Weapon		Establishment, Colchester
Cap GS	Cap, General Service	MBT	Main Battle Tank	SLR	Self-Loading Rifle
CBW	Chemical and Biological	NAAFI	Navy, Army and Air Force	SLTA	Scottish Lowland Training Area
	Warfare		Institutes	SMLE	Short Magazine Lee Enfield
CEFO	Combat Equipment Fighting	NATO	North Atlantic Treaty	SMG	Submachine-gun
	Order		Organization	SUIT	Sight Unit Individual Trilux
CEMO	Combat Equipment Marching	NBC	Nuclear, Biological and Chemical	SUSAT	Sight Unit Small Arms Trilux
	Order	NBCD	Nuclear, Biological and	TA	Territorial Army
CIC	Chief Inspector of Clothing		Chemical Defence	UKLF	United Kingdom Land Forces
DIC	Director of Inspection of	NCO	Non-Commissioned Officer	VCP	Vehicle Check Point
	Clothing (ex-CIC)	OD	Olive Drab (US)	WO	Warrant Officer
DLI	Durham Light Infantry	OG	Olive Green (UK)	WRAC	Women's Royal Army Corps
DMS	Direct Moulded Soles	OR	Other Ranks	WRAF	Women's Royal Air Force

BIBLIOGRAPHY

Barnes, Major R. Money. *A History of the Regiments and Uniforms of the British Army.* Seeley Service, London 1950

Barnes, Major R. Money, and Allen, C. Kennedy. *The Uniforms and History of the Scottish Regiments.* Seeley Service, London 1956

Barthorp, Michael. *British Cavalry Uniforms Since 1660.* Blandford Press, 1984

— *British Infantry Uniforms Since 1660.* Blandford Press, 1982

Beevor, Anthony. *Inside the British Army.* Chatto, 1990

Brereton, J. M. *The British Soldier: A Social History from 1661 to the Present Day.* The Bodley Head, 1986

Chappell, Michael. *The British Army in the 1980s,* Elite Series 14. Osprey, 1987

— *British Infantry Equipment 1908–80,* Men-at-Arms 108. Osprey, 1980

— *The British Soldier in the Twentieth Century.* Wessex Military Publishing: No. 2 *Field Service Head-dress* (1987); No. 3 *Personal Equipment, 1945 to the Present Day* (1987); No. 5 *Battledress 1939–1960* (1988); No. 6 *Tropical Uniforms* (1988)

Carman, W. Y. *A Dictionary of Military Uniform.* Batsford, 1977

— *British Military Uniforms (From Contemporary Pictures) Henry VIII to Present Day.* Leonard Hill

Cochrane, Peter. *Scottish Military Dress.* Blandford Press, 1987

Jewell, Brian, and Chappell, Michael (illust.). *British Battledress 1937–61, Men-at-Arms 112. Osprey, 1981*

Mollo, Andrew, and MacGregor, Malcolm (illust.). *Army Uniforms of World War 2.* Blandford Press, 1973

Scurr, John, and Chappell, Michael (illust.). *The Malayan Campaign 1948–60,* Men-at-Arms 132. Osprey, 1982

Smith, Major Digby G., and Chappell, Michael. *Army Uniforms Since 1945.* Blandford Press, 1980

Smith, Major Digby G., and McBride, Angus (illust.). *The British Army 1965–80,* Men-at-Arms 71. Osprey, 1977

Stanhope, Henry. *The Soldiers, An Anatomy of the British Army.* Hamish Hamilton, 1979

Thompson, Leroy, and Chappell, Michael (illust.). *Uniforms of the Elite Forces.* Blandford Press, 1982

Wise, Terence. *A Guide to Military Museums.* Athena Books, 1969–1990

Wood, Stephen. *The Scottish Soldier.* Archive Publications Ltd in association with National Museums of Scotland

Official Publications
Army Orders (various years)
Clothing Regulations, various pamphlets (various years)
Dress Regulations for Officers of the Army (various years)
Material Regulations (various years)
Officers' Dress Regulations. The Royal Scots [The Royal Regiment] (various years)
Uniforms for the Services. CISC, 1939